ONLI... ...ABASE

SEARC... ...BRARIES

DATE DUE

Demco, Inc. 38-293

1992

ASSOCIATION OF

COLLEGE

& RESEARCH

LIBRARIES

A DIVISION OF THE
AMERICAN LIBRARY ASSOCIATION

Published by the Association of College and Research Libraries
A Division of the American Library Association
50 East Huron Street
Chicago, IL 60611-2795

ISBN: 0-8389-7651-4

This publication is printed on recycled paper with vegetable based ink.

TABLE OF CONTENTS

CLIP NOTES COMMITTEE

James Cubit, Chair
Williams College

Dan Bedsole
Randolph Macon College

Patricia S. Butcher
Trenton State College

Ray English
Oberlin College

Andrea C. Hoffman
Wheelock College

Lawrie Merz
Houghton College

Allen S. Morrill
Kansas City Art Institute

INTRODUCTION

Many changes have occurred in the information environment since 1983 when the ACRL College Libraries Section published <u>CLIP Note</u> #4, "Online Bibliographic Database Searching in College Libraries". Use of online searching has expanded, the library electronic landscape has evolved dramatically with the advent of Compact-Disc Read-Only-Memory (CD-ROM) databases and online public access catalogs (OPACs) serve increasingly as gateways to a multitude of other databases. Considering these advances, it is clearly time for an updated picture of the electronic scene in libraries. This <u>College Library Information Packet (CLIP) Note</u> on computer-based database services in college libraries provides a much needed update

Objectives of the Study

The function of <u>CLIP Notes</u> is to publish basic data and sample documents that college libraries can use in establishing, evaluating or refining their specific services or operations. Thus, our objective in this study was to determine the extent to which college libraries are offering CD-ROM and online bibliographic database searching services, either as separate stand-alone services or through other means such as online catalog gateways. We also wished to collect samples of policies and procedure statements, forms, public relations documents and instructional handouts that would be beneficial to libraries in offering online search, CD-ROM and other computer-based services.

Survey Sample and Methodology

In order to provide a representative sample of college libraries, the compilers utilized groupings established by the Carnegie Foundation for the Advancement of Teaching. Institutions were selected from two groups from the Carnegie list: Comprehensive Universities and Colleges I, and Liberal Arts College I. Most of these institutions have an enrollment of less than 1,000 FTE undergraduate students. The result is a sample of 260 college and university libraries located throughout the nation.

The survey was sent to the 260 library directors in April of 1991, with a return date of June 15 requested. A follow-up postcard inquiry was sent out to libraries who had not responded. Final response totaled 179 completed surveys for a 68.8% return rate.

Survey Findings

The survey confirms what the professional literature and conference themes suggest; the college library has entered seriously into the electronic age. Not only is the use of electronic sources very widespread, but the breadth of sources provided has expanded rapidly as new services have become available. College libraries are taking full advantage of the expanding information industry. On the other hand, the vision of the library without walls, one in which library-administered electronic sources are distributed outside the library, has come to fruition in few cases. Another striking development is the inclusion of electronic information sources in bibliographic instruction; clearly, computer-based resources are being integrated heavily into the instruction that is becoming a central service in college libraries today. A review of particular elements of the survey results follows.

Among the responding institutions, online services are almost universally available. In 1983, 65% of the respondents offered this service; now 95% do so. The budgetary commitment to online searching is fairly consistent, with the largest percentage of libraries (39%) expending between $1000 and $3999 annually on such searching. Only two libraries who offered the service indicated that it was entirely fee-based, another indicator of the assumption that online searching is a core service. Dialog is by far the most heavily used vendor; 86% of respondents subscribe to Dialog. The next most-used vendor was BRS at 27%. Although all but two libraries provide online searching through intermediaries in the reference department, only 24 (14%) evaluate the performance of intermediate searchers in any way.

1

Responses to questions concerning CD-ROMs indicate that CD-ROM searching is now offered more prevalently than online searching was offered in 1983; 90% of respondents have some form of CD-ROM product. Considering the short history of the availability of CD-ROM technology, this seems an extremely quick application of new technology across a wide array of college libraries. The financial commitment to CD-ROM is greater than that for online searching; the largest group of libraries (32%) are spending from $4,000 to $6,999 per year on CD-ROM subscriptions. Equipment purchases are another obstacle to implementing CD-ROM and online services; libraries seem to be spending slowly in this area with the largest group of responding libraries reporting that they have spent less than $4,999 over the past five years for both online and CD-ROM hardware (55% for online-supporting hardware and 30% for CD-ROM).

By far the most popular CD-ROM title is ERIC; 70 of the 153 libraries that provide CD-ROM services subscribe to ERIC. Next to ERIC comes the Academic Index in various forms at 56 (36%). The various Wilson indexes represent a large number of the next most prevalent group of titles.

An inquiry regarding the popularity of CD-ROMs relative to paper indexes brought a resounding 97% (139) who saw CD as more popular (Question 16). This popularity raises the issue of whether paper indexes are being cancelled once CDs are purchased (Question 14). College libraries seem to be being quite conservative in their approach to this issue; 113 (72%) had not yet cancelled any paper indexes. On the other hand, several respondents made it clear that they were seriously considering such cancellations: "in process of evaluation" was the response from 13 libraries. The much touted local area networks to make CD-ROM databases available at multiple workstations were not heavily in use; only 5 libraries (3%) reported such usage. Off-site campus networking was mentioned for CD-ROM access in only two cases. In those cases this use was reported as projected rather than actual.

Computer-based public access catalogs represent a much larger one-time investment in both funds and staff implementation time than either CD-ROM data bases or online searching. It is not surprising, therefore, that OPACs are less prevalent than either online searching or CD-ROM services. Ninety-nine (57%) of college libraries who responded were on OPACs. The vendors of these systems were distributed fairly broadly; of the 26 systems identified, the top system had 11 installations (Library Corporation's Intelligent Catalog) and was followed closely by several other vendors with between 7 and 10 installations. No one seems to have sewn up the college library OPAC market at the time in which the survey was conducted, and there are many installations yet to be done. Online systems dominate the market, with only 14% on CD-ROM or laserdisc formats. Monographs are included in all 99 of the respondents' catalogs, other formats represented include serials (54), microforms (68), government documents (58) and media (78). Few libraries reported that their OPACs function as gateways to other databases.

Questions about instruction, promotion, and access were asked about all three types of electronic information sources (online searching, CD-ROMs and public access catalogs). College libraries are using every available opportunity to promote use, publicize services, and teach patrons. One avenue for instruction that was not identified (questions 8, 18, 21) in the options which respondents referred to often was the inclusion of electronic services in bibliographic instruction. In the case of online services, BI was mentioned by few (7) libraries but about 20 libraries added notes to their responses indicating that bibliographic instruction was used to promote and teach patrons to use CD-ROM services and the public catalog. If users do have direct access to online services, the most common form of instruction is one-to-one personal interaction.

Libraries use a variety of means to keep up with the many products on the market, determine what to buy, and decide how to develop and maintain searching skills. For online services, vendor programs (138), professional literature (157), and conference exhibits (119) are important sources of information, although 8 libraries maintain that they "do not remain current"! For CD products, selection is informed significantly by a variety of sources; conference exhibits, product reviews, advertisements, and the recommendations of other librarians were all noted by more than 100 libraries as information sources for CD ROM selection.

In summary, online searching and CD-ROM services are widespread in college libraries, while computer-based catalogs are becoming common but not universal. Instruction and promotion of CD-ROM and OPAC services are well integrated with library instruction for paper sources. Online searching, meanwhile, remains a librarian-mediated service or an individually taught skill. Electronic information sources have not yet been widely distributed beyond the library, and college libraries are still loath to part with their paper indexes despite the popularity of CD-ROM alternatives.

Description of Documents

Libraries responding to the survey were asked to submit sample documents relating to online and CD-ROM database searching. Many excellent documents were received. However, some of the documents submitted could not be included in this CLIP Note as they could not be easily reproduced in the required format. A large number of instructional guides and other materials promoting the use of online catalogs was also received. However, since few of these documents contained information on searching online databases (via gateways or other means) they were not included. The documents that have been included are intended to serve as examples that can aid libraries in designing documentation for online and CD-ROM searching programs of their own.

Acknowledgements

There were many who gave their time and expertise to make this publication possible. The CLIP Notes Committee was extremely helpful throughout. Tom Freeman was responsible for final word processing. The many libraries and librarians who contributed were, of course, the core of the project.

Finally, this monograph is dedicated to the memory of Cheryl Thurston, Evergreen State College Library Administrative Assistant, who formatted the survey, did the mailings and began the survey compilation before being overtaken by illness.

Works Cited

Carnegie Foundation for the Advancement of Teaching. A Classification of Institutions of Higher Education. Princeton, NJ: Carengie Foundation for the Advancement of Teaching, 1987.

SURVEY RESULTS

General Library Characteristics

1) a. Number of full-time equivalent (FTE) undergraduate students:

37	(21%)	under 1,000
92	(52%)	1,000-1,999 FTE
35	(20%)	2,000-2,999 FTE
12	(7%)	3,000-3,999 FTE
1	(1%)	4,000-4,999 FTE
1	(1%)	5,000 and over FTE

Total: 178

b. Number of full-time equivalent (FTE) graduate students:

69	(39%)	no graduate students
69	(39%)	under 200
31	(17%)	200-499 FTE
8	(4%)	500-799 FTE
0	(0%)	800-1,000 FTE
1	(1%)	over 1,000 FTE

Total: 178

2) a. Total library collection count in volumes (including bound periodicals, microforms, and government documents):

2	(1%)	less than 50,000
11	(6%)	50,000-100,000
74	(42%)	100,001-200,000
37	(21%)	200,001-300,000
19	(11%)	300,001-400,000
14	(8%)	400,001-500,000
7	(4%)	500,001-600,000
12	(7%)	600,001+

Total: 176

b. Total library reference collection count in volumes (including government documents):

27	(20%)	0-5,000 volumes
63	(46%)	5,001-10,000
28	(21%)	10,001-20,000
8	(6%)	20,001-30,000
10	(7%)	30,001+

Total: 136

5

3) a. Annual library acquisition budget for monographs:

38	(21%)	under $49,999
73	(41%)	$50,000-$99,999
33	(18%)	$100,000-$149,999
35	(20%)	$150,000 and over

Total: 179

b. Annual acquisition budget for serials subscriptions:

54	(31%)	under $49,999
68	(38%)	$50,000-$99,999
22	(12%)	$100,000-$149,000
33	(19%)	$150,000 and over

Total: 177

c. Annual acquisition budget for CD-ROM subscriptions:

19	(11%)	$0
11	(6%)	under $1,000
30	(17%)	$1000-$3,999
56	(32%)	$4,000-$6,999
34	(20%)	$7,000-$9,999
24	(14%)	$10,000 and over

Total: 155

d. Annual budget for online bibliographic search service charges (such as are available through DIALOG or are locally mounted, but excluding OPACs):

8	(5%)	$0
46	(26%)	under $1,000
69	(39%)	$1000-$3,999
28	(16%)	$4,000-$6,999
11	(6%)	$7,000-$9,999
11	(6%)	$10,000 and over
2	(1%)	$0 (fee-based)

Total: 175

4) a. Total amount invested since 1985 in library hardware for online database retrieval services:

20	(11%)	$0
95	(55%)	under $4,999
43	(25%)	$5,000-$9,999
8	(5%)	$10,000-$14,999
5	(3%)	$15,000-$19,999
3	(2%)	$20,000 and over

Total: 174

b. Total amount invested since 1985 in software for searching online databases (such as is necessary for mounting local databases or for communication with remote databases --but excluding OPACs):

35	(20%)	$0
130	(75%)	under $4,999
7	(4%)	$5,000-$9,999
1	(1%)	$10,000-$14,999
0	(0%)	$15,000-$19,999
1	(1%)	$20,000 and over

Total: 174

5) a. Total amount invested since 1985 in library hardware for searching CD-ROM databases:

19	(11%)	$0
52	(30%)	under $4,999
51	(29%)	$5,000-$9,999
27	(15%)	$10,000-$14,999
14	(8%)	$15,000-$19,999
12	(7%)	$20,000 and over

Total: 175

b. Total amount invested in software since 1985 for searching CD-ROM systems, including subscription fees:

17	(10%)	$0
50	(29%)	under $4,999
45	(26%)	$5,000-$9,999
17	(18%)	$10,000-$14,999
24	(14%)	$15,000-$19,999
21	(12%)	$20,000 and over

Total: 174

c. Percentage of total 1989/90 annual acquisition budget devoted to CD-ROM software:

21	(13%)	0%
15	(10%)	up to 1%
25	(16%)	1% to 2%
25	(16%)	2+ to 3%
15	(10%)	3+ to 4%
22	(14%)	4+ to 5%
7	(4%)	5+ to 6%
4	(3%)	6+ to 7%
5	(3%)	7+ to 8%
3	(2%)	8+ to 9%
9	(6%)	9+ to 10%
5	(3%)	over 10%

Total: 156

Online Bibliographic Search Services

6. Do you offer online bibliographic search services (such as DIALOG)?

   168   (95%)   Yes

                Vendors:

144	Dialog
46	BRS
36	EPIC
28	STN
27	Wilsonline
9	Datatimes
8	Easynet
8	RLIN
8	VuText
5	OCLC
4	Dow Jones News Net
4	Knowledge Index
4	Medlars
2	CAS
2	NEXIS
2	ORBIT
2	Veralek

      1   each: CANO, Chemical Abstracts, Compuserve, Dowline, EBB, FAPRS, Grateful Med,IAC (via CARL), Infoglobe, Legislate, LEXIS, Medline, NCJDB, NLM, ORION, Passport, Prism, Profile, State of Oregon newspapers, Telebase Systems, Westlaw

      6   Vendor not specified

    9   (5%)   No

Total: 177

7. Means by which library provides users with access to online databases (respondents checked all that applied):

   166   Service provided by reference department--i.e., delegated searches through intermediary

   32   Direct access through end-user searching. Specific method:

   10   End-user searching limited to specific databases (those mentioned: OCLC, Legislate, Dialog CIP, Easynet, STN College, RLIN, M-PALS, Knowledge Index, Westlaw, Lexis/Nexis, Dow Jones)
   5   Chemistry students only
   4   Faculty only
   2   Terminals in reference
   1   Paralegal students only
   1   Honors students only
   1   In research methods class
   6   Gateway access through OPAC by mounting of commercial databases
   15   Public end-user terminals available in library

2   Other:

    1   Service provided by Technical Services department
    1   CAS in Chemistry department

8. Instructional methods (respondents checked all that applied):

   29   Self-instruction/hands-on experience
   50   One-to-one personal instruction
   27   Point-of-use instructional material
   33   Introductory lecture
   30   Peers, pairs, or small group instruction
    6   Front-end tutorial (computer-based, database specific)

   10   Other:

    7   Included in library instruction (workshops, classes, demonstrations)
    1   Workbook
    1   Brochure
    1   Taught by course faculty

   61   No end-user instruction offered.

9. Promotional activities for online searching (respondents checked all that applied):

  162   Referral from the reference desk
   32   Promotional signage
   64   Communication with faculty
   35   Articles in school newspaper

   62   Other:

    31   Bibliographic instruction
    11   Campus/library newspapers, letters
     9   Brochures, pamphlets, information sheets
     5   Library orientation
     3   Through classes
     1   Faculty retreat
     1   Free searches for graduate students
     1   Library fair

10. Most common methods by which staff increase their knowledge of search products and search strategies (respondents checked all that applied):

  138   Attending seminars by commercial vendors
  157   Reading the professional literature
    7   Attending refresher courses in library school
  119   Viewing products at conference exhibits
    8   Do not remain current

   48   Other:

    13   Learn from colleagues, in-house training
    12   Seminars/workshops by local consortia, library organizations, networks
     8   Practice/hands-on work
     1   User groups
     1   Call vendors
     1   Vendor literature
     1   Campus computing staff
     1   Chronolog

11. Is the performance of intermediary searchers evaluated?

   24   (14%) Yes

      How:

6	User questionnaire/evaluation form
3	Use statistics
2	User feedback
2	Billings/budget
2	End results
2	MBWA (management by walking around)
2	By director
1	Annual circulation
1	Annual performance review
1	Informally
1	Self-evaluation
1	By searcher and client
1	Interview patron
1	Spot-check

  145 (85%) No

Compact Disc-Read Only Memory (CD-ROM)

12. Do you offer CD-ROM databases (other than public access catalogs)?

  153 (90%) Yes

      Products:

70	ERIC (various vendors)
56	Academic Index (includes Expanded version)
42	Psychlit
33	Humanities Index
37	Government Publications (Various vendors)
27	Modern Language Association Bibliography
27	Social Science Index
24	Books in Print
24	Infotrac
21	BPI
20	General Science Index
17	Readers' Guide
15	CINAHL
14	PAIS
12	ABI Inform
12	Religion Indexes
11	Newsbank
10	Compact Disclosure
10	Periodical Abstracts
10	Sociofile
9	Infotrac Business
9	National newspaper Index
9	Wilson (no specific titles given)

8	Econlit
7	Newspaper abstracts
7	Medline
6	Newspaper index
6	UMI (no specific titles given)
5	Government depository service titles
5	Shakespeare
5	Ulrichs
89	other titles mentioned four or fewer times

17   (10%) No

13. Information sources for selection of CD-ROM products obtained (respondents checked all that applied):

87	Demonstration by salespeople
112	Exhibits at conferences
135	Product reviews
109	Publishers' advertisements
109	Other librarians' recommendation

32   Other:

20	Trial demonstration periods
2	Faculty recommendations
2	Library school
2	Use of on-line version
2	Use at other libraries
1	Use at regional workshops
1	Had to select least expensive products
1	Comparison to print versions
1	High use of print versions

14. Have you cancelled paper counterparts for any of the CD-ROM tools?

113   (72%) No

Why?

50	Need back-up when CD's are busy or down
30	Does not directly replace any paper titles
17	Need to assure complete back file
13	In process of evaluation
9	User/librarian resistance
9	No savings would result
4	Paper still heavily used
3	Some different/more efficient searching provided by paper
2	In order to teach both formats
2	Currency
1	Incomplete/erroneous data
1	Unsure

43   (28%) Yes

11

<u>Why?</u>

19	Expense
15	Replication
8	CD easier to use
6	Paper no longer used
3	CD more comprehensive
2	Space
1	Patrons won't use paper anymore
1	Ties in with CD-ROM OPAC
1	No more fiche filing
1	"Isn't it obvious?"

15. Promotional activities for CD-ROM products (respondents checked all that applied):

158	Referral from the reference desk
112	Promotional signage
144	Communication with faculty
53	Articles in school newspaper

<u>Other</u>:

71	Bibliographic instruction (various formats)
15	College/library newsletters, letters, memos
10	Handouts, brochures, fliers, etc.
7	Word-of-mouth
2	Faculty assignments/English instruction
1	Location
1	Faculty meeting announcements
1	Freshman library workbook
1	Faculty/staff seminars
1	Student library assistants' direction

16. Have you detected any preference among users for CD-ROM rather than paper tools?

5	(3%)	No preference detected
139	(97%)	Yes

<u>If yes, how do you regulate usage?</u>

32	Time limit
28	Not necessary yet
23	We don't
17	First come, first served
15	No comment
11	Encourage use of alternative sources
11	Sign-up sheet
10	Queue-driven
7	Schedule longer searches
3	Limit printing
2	Staff monitoring
1	Programmed time-out
1	Data bases mounted individually
1	LAN provides plenty of access

17. Have you detected any preference among users for menu or command-driven searches?

    42   (28%)   Menu
          Comments: convenience, only access available (2), easier (16), less intimidating, preferred at first, we teach that way, less time consuming, good for casual users (2).

    8   (8%)   Command
          Comments: more powerful, advanced users prefer, users are more intelligent than CD menus give credit for, menus slow our students down.

    43   (29%)   Don't know

    57   (38%)   No preference detected

18. Instructional methods used for CD-ROM services (Respondents checked all that applied):

    51   Self-instruction/hands-on experience
    52   One-to-one personal instruction
    117   Point-of-need instructional material
    105   Introductory lecture
    115   Peer instruction (informal or formal)
    32   Front-end tutorial (computer-based, database specific)

    Other:

        23   Bibliographic instruction (various formats)
        2   Handouts/brochures
        1   Individualized search sessions

19. Ways users access CD-ROM databases:

    158   (95%) At library workstations
    5   (3%) Through local area networks

    Vendors:

        1   Optinet
        1   Silverplatter
        1   IRSM token ring & local gateway
        1   Lantastic

    4   (2%) Other:
          2   Reference desk intermediary
          2   Off-site via campus network (soon)

Online Public Access Catalog (OPAC)

20. a. Have you implemented an online public access catalog (OPAC) or a CD-ROM public access catalog?

99   (57%) Yes

Medium

78   (79%) Online
14   (14%) CD-Rom
7   (7%) No medium specified

Vendors:

10   Innovative Interfaces
11   Library Corporation Intelligent Catalog
9   Dynix
8   DRA
7   VTLS
4   CLSI
4   LS2000
3   NOTIS
3   Marcive
3   UNISYS/PALS
2   Ameritec
2   Carlyle
2   Marmot/CARL
3   Illinet
2   Geac
2   MultiLIS
1   each: Autographics, DMO, LIS (Library Information System),
         SIRSI, CARL, Laserguide, UTLAS, LePac, Inlex,
         Blue Star Library System)

76   (43%) No

b. Formats of information available through the computer-based catalog:

100   Monographs
65   Serials
68   Microforms
58   Government documents
78   Media/nonprint:
33   Video
23   Records
15   CD's
12   Audio cassettes
8   Audio tapes
7   Films
5   Kits
5   Filmstrips
1   Games
1   Models

14

22 Other:

    7 Various databases
    3 Scores
    1 each: Wilson indexes, CD-ROM's, maps, pamphlets,
        prints, a-v equipment, union catalog, vertical file, archives, music, manuscripts, laserdiscs

21. Instructional methods for computer-based catalogs (respondents checked all that applied):

    91 Self-instruction/hands-on experience
    91 One-to-one personal instruction
    83 Point-of-use instructional material
    72 Introductory lecture
    57 Peers, pairs, or small group instruction
    13 Front-end tutorial (computer-based, database specific)

    26 Other:

        19 Bibliographic instruction (various formats)
        1   Distribution of basic instructions
        1   Faculty staff seminars
        1   Library workbook requirement
        1   Brochures
    3 No end user instruction is provided

22. Promotional activities for catalog (respondents checked all that applied):

    94 Referral from the reference desk
    52 Promotional signage
    82 Communication with faculty
    52 Articles in school newspaper
    34 Library newsletter

Other:

    21 Bibliographic instruction (various formats)
    6 Catalog is closed; no choice
    3 Promotes itself
    2 Remote access
    2 Handouts
    1 Library handbook
    1 Building design
    1 Academic computing center newsletter
    1 Instructions for faculty
    1 Campus newsletter

    2 No end user instruction is provided

23. Additional Comments:

Instruction/promotion:

"Have found students bright -- already know computers and search strategies; teach themselves and one another."

"Our OPAC very user-friendly with on-line authority file for author/corporate author/uniform title/subject to allow patrons to locate materials even without proper terminology."

"Don't find promotion of electronic services necessary."

CD-ROM:

"Plan to expand CD-ROM holdings."

"CD-ROM % of budget increasing."

"Hope to add new CD-ROM tools and hope the additions will cause students to be more critical in selection of tools."

Other:

"OPAC acquired through regional cooperation."

"Adding UMI's periodicals database to OPAC, Fall 1991."

"Target completion RECON 2-4 years."

ONLINE BIBLIOGRAPHIC

SEARCHING DOCUMENTS

POLICY STATEMENTS

Dickinson College Library

DATABASE SEARCHING POLICY

The Library is committed to providing the Dickinson College community with subsidized online database searching to the greatest extent that our budget can support. Our funds for doing so, however are limited. Therefore, in order to increase the equitable distribution of pay-for-use online services to Dickinson users, the following guidelines shall be observed in serving student, faculty, administrative, and non-campus community users.

Students: The library will support student research projects up to $50 per year per student in subsidized search time. In order to promote research skills among students, the library will also fund demonstrations or live searches as part of our bibliographic instruction in freshman seminars and lower level classes as deemed appropriate by the librarian.

Individual Faculty, Academic Professionals and Administrators: The library will support online services for individual research up to $50 per person per year. Research, as used in this context, does not include tenure or contract review or similar activities.

Departmental and Administrative Users: Online services performed for academic departments in support of curriculum development research will be billed to the department. Online services provided in support of research conducted on behalf of an administrative office will be billed to that office. Individuals who receive research grants are encouraged to budget funds for online services into their grant proposals.

Non-Dickinson Users: All online services performed for individuals who are not members of the Dickinson College community will be billed to the individual. An additional fee of $10 will be charged in addition to the online charges to cover administrative costs. As a general rule, the library does not extend online search services to for-profit corporations; however, local and Dickinson-related businesses will be given special consideration.

Helpful Hints for All Users

1. Please allow ample time for us to complete the search. The librarian performing the search may need to do some background research or discuss the topic with you before-hand.
2. It is often helpful if you can be present when the search is performed, to help evaluate the results and refine the search, if necessary.
3. Since not all areas of research are covered by online databases and online services may not be appropriate for all search requests, the librarian may recommend the use of printed indexes, rather than online services.
4. Reminder: When you write R & D requests or grant proposals to include a sum for online searching.

Dulaney-Browne Library   9-90
2501 N. Blackwelder
Oklahoma City, OK 73106

Oklahoma
City University

POLICY

ONLINE DATABASE SEARCHING

The Dulaney Browne Library is pleased to offer online database searching. In order for the experience to be a positive one for all concerned, the following policies will be followed:

1. We will do searches for administrators, faculty, staff, and graduate students.

2. Friends card holders as residents of Oklahoma City have access to $20.00 free searching per month through the Metropolitan Library System and should plan to use that service.

3. Undergraduate students have access to the service only on the recommendation of a faculty member.

4. The determination of whether or not an online database search is needed will be made by librarians. There are occasions when a manual search will be as productive as an online search.

5. Only staff of the Dulaney Browne Library will have access to the equipment and the password. We realize that many people are skilled database searchers and we respect their expertise. However, the responsibility for balancing the library budget rests with library personnel. For this reason, the control of the costs must remain with library personnel as well.

6. The library will pay for the first $20.00 of searches for faculty and graduate students. The patron will be expected to pay the remainder of the charges. This money will be due at the completion of the search.

AUTOMATED DATABASE SEARCHING POLICY

General Guidelines

1. **Reference staff should be able to effectively use the search software of the online and CDROM systems currently available to the Joint Libraries.**

   Online systems currently that are currently available include Dialog, BRS AfterDark, Datatimes, EPIC, LUMINA, and PALS. CDROM systems include WilsonDisc (both Browse and Wilsearch search modes) and Marcive for government documents. In the future, we are likely to have additional CDROM products from other vendors.

2. **Reference staff should provide quick reference searches on demand using online databases and CDROM.**

   Quick reference searches are defined as simple bibliographic verifications, or author and subject searches that result in 10 or less citations and a simple search strategy usually using only one or two search terms and basic proximity or Boolean operators.

3. **Reference staff should utilize automated searching in the routine provision of reference services, identify user needs and make appropriate referrals for complex searches.**

   Complex searches are defined as anything beyond a quick reference search, requiring more than one or two terms and a simple search strategy with a general target of more than 10 citations.

Specifics and Definitions

1. **Designated searchers**

   Volunteers from the reference staff will handle referrals for complex searches. Insofar as possible, the various subject disciplines will be divided among the volunteers so that some in-depth knowledge of specific databases can be attained. These searchers will also act as consultants and, when appropriate, provide training workshops.

2. **Charges to the user**

   Quick reference searches are provided to users at no cost. In addition, searches on Dissertation Abstracts are free to all users. For complex searches, the charges vary by the database vendor used:

BRS AfterDark
$3.00 per search or 2/3's actual cost, whichever is
greater.

Dialog
Full cost passed on to the user.

Datatimes
Free access to Star and Tribune, including displays
of header information. Charges for all other use,
including full-text of Star and Tribune articles and
searches of other newspaper databases or information
services, are passed on to the user.

EPIC
Full cost passed on to the user.

LUMINA
Free to the user.

PALS
Free to the user.

Of course, these charges are subject to professional
judgement in cases of hardware, software, or search
strategy malfunctions.

3. **Eligible users**

All members of our local academic and monastic community
are eligible for online database searches, including
faculty spouses and alumni. Except for those who wish to
use the government documents collection, all
non-affiliates will be referred to SCSU or GRRL.

4. **Scheduling**

Quick reference searches, as noted above, should be
performed on demand. Insofar as possible, complex
searches will also be available on demand. In many cases,
however, a referral will be made and an appointment set up
with the appropriate searcher. Users will be consulted as
to the immediacy of their need and willingness to pay a
higher rate for a Dialog search compared to a BRS
AfterDark search performed on the same database.

5. **Training workshops**

Training workshops will be provided for all appropriate
database vendors (in-house, if possible). Additional
resources are also available, such as free training
seminars offered for specific databases, practice
databases on all the major online vendors, and manuals for
individual sessions.

SAINT JOSEPH'S COLLEGE
RENSSELAER, INDIANA 47978
PHONE 219: 866-7111

SAINT JOSEPH'S COLLEGE LIBRARY

POLICY ON DATA BASE SEARCHES

As part of our library reference service, we are able to search the BRS network of data bases for information. A large number of data bases are available in the following areas: life sciences, physical/applied sciences, medicine/pharmacology, social sciences/humanities, education, business, and reference. Data bases make available online: 1) periodical indexes that we also have available in print, but with more thorough cross-referencing and greater accuracy; 2) periodical indexes and a variety of other informational sources not published in paper format; and 3) cumulated indexes, statistical data and abstracts which we do not have in our collections or which we may eventually have to discontinue because of increasing costs.

If a student or faculty member is conducting research and can't seem to find enough information or the kind of information desired, then he or she should consider having a computer search done. A computer search provides the patron with a bibliography of sources on the topic of interest. Depending upon the individual data base, this bibliography could contain citations to books, periodical articles, government publications, etc. The patron would then check our collection to see if the sources retrieved in the bibliography are available in the library. For those items desired but unavailable, the interlibrary loan service should be considered.

FACULTY: Data base searches will be done free of charge for Saint Joseph's College faculty to assist them in research for course development and classroom work, for scholarly publication, grant preparation and committee work. Because these data bases are expensive, however, we expect that whenever grant monies or other funds are available to a particular faculty member in his or her work that these funds will be used for the telecommunications, online connect charges and printing costs connected with computerized information retrieval. There will be no charge for the searcher's time. The same policy will apply to administrators of the college in matters associated with their work for the college.

STUDENTS: Searching will also be done free of charge to Saint Joseph's College students who are engaged in significant class-related research, provided they have been referred to the searcher by a faculty member or a librarian who has judged that the student has exhausted the available printed sources and that his/her topic is reasonable and appropriate. Many college and university libraries charge students for computerized reference services. In order for the library at SJC to avoid charging for searches, it is important that we be able to determine that a search is necessary.

For students desiring to utilize our BRS service to search data bases for any other reason, there will be a flat fee of $5.00 per search, per data base searched, with offline printout of up to 20 citations. An extra fee of 20 cents per citation will be charged for citations over that number. (All actual costs are not recovered in this charge.)

Faculty, staff or students seeking information that does not relate to our academic and teaching/learning enterprise will be charged the cost of the search (online connect charges, telecommunications, and printing and mailing costs). They will be accommodated at the discretion of the Reference Librarian (other duties and responsibilities permitting).

INDIVIDUALS NOT EMPLOYED BY OR ENROLLED AT THE COLLEGE: In addition to online charges (a $5.00 minimum), a consultant's fee of $10.00 per half hour or portion thereof (e.g. 45 minutes' fee would be $20.00) will be charged. Those not employed by or enrolled at the college will be accommodated at the discretion of the Reference Librarian.

THE SEARCH PROCESS: To apply for a search, the patron must fill out a search form indicating the kinds of citations desired and appropriate subject terminology. These forms are available from the Reference Librarian. The Reference Librarian will then contact the individual to arrange for an interview to set up a search strategy, if necessary. Each data base has its own vocabulary and changing search strategies and data contents, so it is essential that a trained and experienced operator do the searching.

SEARCH PRODUCTS: The Reference Librarian will decide whether it is appropriate to print citations on or off line, with or without abstracts, or with abbreviated citations. The library also reserves the right to keep copies of all search strategies as well as any printed citations. If the librarians share this information with other persons requesting similar searches, the identity of previous searchers will be kept confidential.

Transylvania University Library

DIALOG Searching Guidelines

1. You may request a search by completing a DIALOG Search Request Form.
    These are located at the Information Desk.

2. You should plan on being present for the actual search. If the search
    needs to be narrowed or broadened your presence will avoid delays and
    costly connect time.

3. Two days from the time you complete the Request Form is usually suf-
    ficient notice for an appointment.

4. The cost to Transylvania students, faculty, and staff is $5.00. How-
    ever, community patrons and spouses of Transylvania University
    students, faculty and staff will be charged for the entire cost of
    their searches. Costs normally are $20.00 to $50.00, depending upon
    the databases searched and the length of online time required for the
    searches.

PROMOTIONAL LITERATURE

ONLINE DATABASES

WHAT ARE ONLINE DATABASES?

These are files of information that are accessible through a computer. Many online databases are simply the computer-held equivalents of reference books that we own — *PsychINFO (Psychological Abstracts)* and *The Encyclopedia of Associations* are examples of these — but there are quite a few files which are available to us only in their online format. Online databases can contain either bibliographic citations, as do *Social Sciences Index* and *BIOSIS (Biological Abstracts)*, or non-bibliographical information such as statistics (*BLS Consumer Price Index*) or the names of chemical substances (*Chemname*). The Library currently provides access to more than 300 databases in all fields of research.

WHY WOULD I WANT AN ONLINE DATABASE SEARCH?

There are several reasons why an online search might be useful in your research. The most obvious is that we can search in sources which we don't own in book form — such as *Applied Science and Technology Index* or recent years of *Comprehensive Dissertation Index*. Sometimes finding information on a topic requires using these other reference tools. Also, an online search can combine several diverse concepts and produce a bibliography tailored to your specific research needs. Finally, many online files update more frequently and rapidly than our print indexes.

HOW CAN I REQUEST AN ONLINE SEARCH?

First contact a reference librarian in the Main Library or any of the branch libraries. The librarian will discuss your topic with you, help identify sources of information that we have in the library, and decide whether an online search would be useful. You will then fill out a database search request form, and set up an appointment to have the search done. Since the computer time is expensive, we want to plan the search carefully so that we can do the most efficient search for our money. We can usually schedule an appointment within a day of your request, allowing time for this planning process. At your appointment, we'll go over our plan for the search with you and then do the search. You don't have to be present, but it is recommended; as we start getting responses to the search terms, you can evaluate their usefulness and help redirect the search if necessary. The results of the search may be printed immediately, or we may request that they be printed offline by the vendor and mailed to the library. The option we select will depend on the length of the bibliography, the cost of the database, and how quickly you need the results. It takes approximately 4 business days for search results to arrive by mail, and you'll be notified as soon as they are received.

DOES IT COST ME ANYTHING?

That depends. The service is free for Oberlin College faculty, staff, and students involved in personal academic research on subjects for which an online search would be useful. This can be determined by the librarian as you discuss your topic. Usually, if you are studying the relationship among several concepts, or need to use indexes which are only available online, then a computer search is appropriate. If for some reason the librarian doesn't think an online search would be the best approach, and you still want to request one, we'll be happy to do it, but you will be charged for all search costs. These vary considerably depending on the length of your search and the databases searched. The costs of online searches supporting research for administrative departments normally will be charged back to those departments. Patrons not affiliated with the college may also request a search; they will be charged for all the costs of the search.

WHAT ARE SOME OF THE DATABASES AVAILABLE?

Space does not permit anything but the briefest list of databases. The following list represents the variety and range of topics covered by the online files we can search. Contact a reference librarian for information on additional databases.

Agricola — provides international coverage of journal and monographic literature in agriculture and related fields

Art Index — indexes articles in nearly 200 periodicals in the areas of art, architecture, art history, archaeology, photography, city planning, and related subjects

Arts & Humanities Citation Index — indexes articles in the international journal literature of the humanities and the fine and performing arts

Biography Master Index — accesses biographical information, found in over 700 sources, on both historical and living individuals

Biosis Previews — provides comprehensive worldwide coverage of research in the life sciences

CA Search — indexes the international chemical literature covered in *Chemical Abstracts*

Disclosure Financials — contains extracts of reports filed with the SEC by publicly owned companies

D & B — Dun's Electronic Yellow Pages — provides brief directory information about thousands of U.S. businesses, services, and professionals

Energyline — indexes material on scientific, socio-economic, and policy aspects of energy

Foreign Trade & Econ Abstracts — abstracts journal articles, books, and reports in the fields of economic science and management

Grants — lists grants available through government, foundation, and commercial sources

Legal Resource Index — indexes legal information in law periodicals and monographs

Mathsci — abstracts 1600 mathematical research journals from around the world, equivalent to *Mathematical Reviews*

Medline — covers virtually every subject in the broad field of biomedicine

Microcomputer Index — abstracts articles, new product descriptions, and reviews of software and books from over 50 microcomputer journals

MLA Bibliography — indexes books and periodical articles about languages, literature, linguistics, and folklore

National Newspaper Index — provides comprehensive indexing for the *New York Times, Washington Post, Christian Science Monitor, Los Angeles Times,* and the *Wall Street Journal*

Philosopher's Index — abstracts books and journals covering all aspects of philosophy and related fields

RILM Abstracts — abstracts significant journal literature on all aspects of music

SciSearch — provides author, title keyword, and cited author access to articles in nearly 3,000 scientific and technical journals

ALG, CHC 6/88 rev.

Our Lady of the Lake University of San Antonio

DIALOG COMPUTER SEARCHES

DIALOG computer searches are intended for upper-division and graduate student. <u>There is a charge for this service</u> (see below). For free database searches, see the handout "WILSEARCH COMPUTER SEARCHES".

WHAT IS DIALOG?

DIALOG is the trade name for an online database service. There are over 200 databases available to search in education, psychology, sociology, history, the humanities, life and medical sciences.

Most of the databases do not provide the final information but rather provide a list of citations to articles, reports, proceedings, dissertations, etc. Most databases have a print equivalent.

WHAT ARE THE ADVANTAGES OF A DIALOG SEARCH?

A computer can combine subject terms for two or more concepts to retrieve more precisely the most relevant citations.

Databases are often more current than their printed counterparts.

Many users find it more convenient and faster to do their research using computerized databases.

WHAT WILL YOUR SEARCH RESULTS LOOK LIKE?

You will receive a printout of citations indicating author, title, source and generally an abstract. The printout will **not** contain the entire article.

HOW MUCH DOES A SEARCH COST?

Charges vary depending upon the database searched, telecommunications costs, the amount of computer connect time used, the number of citations received, and the complexity of the topic searched. Typical search charges range from $10 to $40. Non-OLLU patrons are charged an additional $20. Payment may be made by cash or check payable to OLLU.

HOW LONG DOES A SEARCH TAKE?

Most searches can be done within 15-30 minutes, if a librarian is available. Short bibliographies are usually printed during the search. For longer bibliographies, it is more cost effective to print citations offline: in these cases bibliographies are usually available in five working days.

HOW DO I GET A COMPUTER SEARCH RUN?

Tell the librarian at the reference desk that you'd like to do a DIALOG search. We will discuss with you the appropriateness of your topic for a computer search and help you define your search terms. In most cases your search can be run immediately.

SEE OTHER SIDE FOR DATABASE DESCRIPTIONS 33

Our Lady of the Lake University of San Antonio

MOST FREQUENTLY SEARCHED DATABASES AT OLLU

Subject	Database & Description

Business   **ABI/INFORM** is the best database to retrieve articles in business, management and economics. It stresses general decision sciences information which is applicable to many types of businesses and industries. Approximately 550 primary publications in business and related fields. Abstracts included.

Education   **ERIC** covers the field of education with emphasis on American materials. Consists of two files: Resources in Education, which identifies unpublished research reports and projects on microfiche; and Current Index to Journals in Education, an index of more than 700 periodicals in every segment of the education professions. Abstracts included. **Now available at no charge on CD-ROM. See the handout "CD-ROM Computer Searches".**

Medicine   **Medline** is a comprehensive international index of about 3200 journals and selected monographs in the areas of clinical medicine, biomedicine, nursing, and dentistry. Not all items are abstracted.

Psychology   **Psycinfo** is a comprehensive, international, multi-disciplinary database of psychology related materials. Over 900 periodicals and 1500 books, technical reports and monographs are scanned each year to provide coverage of research, theory, and case studies. Abstracts included. **Now available at no charge on CD-ROM. See the handout "CD-ROM Computer Searches".**

Psychology   **Social Scisearch** offers the unique information retrieval technique of search an author's cited references. Over 1,500 social sciences journals throughout the world are indexed.

Sociology   **Sociological Abstracts** provides international coverage of all sociology related disciplines. Over 1200 journals and other serial publications scanned to provide coverage of research, reviews, conference reports, case studies, etc. Abstracts included.

Our Lady of the Lake University of San Antonio

WILSEARCH
COMPUTER SEARCHES

Our Lady
of the Lake
University
f San Antonio

Wilsearch computer searches are intended for OLLU undergraduate student research. This service is limited to OLLU students, faculty and staff. There is a no charge for this service.

WHAT IS WILSEARCH?

Wilsearch is the trade name for an online database service. There are 16 databases available to search in popular literature, business, law, science, technology, biology, education, art, humanities and social sciences. Most databases have a print equivalent.

Wilsearch allows retrieval of citations to articles and books. It does not provide the final information and not all citations will be available at the OLLU libraries.

WHAT ARE THE ADVANTAGES OF WILSEARCH?

Wilsearch can combine subject terms for two or more concepts to retrieve more precisely the most relevant citations.

Wilsearch databases are often more current than their printed counterparts.

Many users find it more convenient and faster to do their research using computerized databases.

WHAT WILL YOUR SEARCH RESULTS LOOK LIKE?

You will receive a printout of citations indicating author, title, and source. The printout will not contain the entire article. Not all citations will be available at the OLLU libraries.

HOW LONG DOES A SEARCH TAKE?

Most searches can be done within 15-30 minutes, if a librarian is available.

HOW DO I GET A COMPUTER SEARCH RUN?

Tell the librarian at the reference desk that you'd like to do a Wilsearch computer search. We will discuss with you the appropriateness of your topic for a computer search and help you define search terms.

SEE OTHER SIDE FOR WILSEARCH DATABASE DESCRIPTIONS

Our Lady of the Lake University of San Antonio

SELECTED WILSEARCH DATABASES

ART INDEX
Art, archaeology, architecture, city planning design, motion
pictures, museum studies and photography.

APPLIED SCIENCE AND TECHNOLOGY INDEX
Engineering, chemistry, mathematics, physics, computer
technology, data processing, and related disciplines.

BIOLOGY AND AGRICULTURE INDEX
Biology, agriculture, biochemistry, environmental science,
ecology, microbiology, and nutrition.

BUSINESS PERIODICALS INDEX
Management, marketing, economics, transportation, computers, as
well as specific industries, businesses, and trades.

EDUCATION INDEX
Pre-school, elementary, secondary, higher, adult, vocational,
continuing, special, physical and religious education; teaching
methods, administration.

GENERAL SCIENCE INDEX
Physical, life, and health sciences, and includes astronomy,
earth science, conservation, nutrition and oceanography.

HUMANITIES INDEX
Archaeology, classical studies, folklore, area studies, history,
language, literature, performing arts, philosophy, religion, and
theology.

INDEX TO LEGAL PERIODICALS
Corporate law, labor relations, taxation, real estate law, estate
planning, and criminal law. Includes statutes and case notes.

LIBRARY LITERATURE
All aspects of librarianship, information science, the book
industry, and publishing.

READERS' GUIDE TO PERIODICAL LITERATURE
Popular literature. Includes current events, business, fashion,
politics, crafts, food, education, sports, history, and science.

SOCIAL SCIENCES INDEX
Interdisciplinary social sciences, and includes economics,
politics, international affairs, anthropology, psychology , and
sociology.

On-Line

REFERENCE

Service

WHAT IS IT?

You probably are familiar with printed indexes used to locate articles from magazines. Think of having these indexes stored in a computer. They would then be referred to as databases. Database searching from a computer terminal can provide information quickly and inexpensively.

ADVANTAGES

Saving time is an important feature of computer searching, but it can also be much more comprehensive than a manual search. Printed indexes limit you to subjects set by the producer of the index. Computer searching can be more creative in that it allows you to use words such as personal names, titles, abstracts, and other components of the topic as well as subject index terms. They may all be combined or limited in various ways according to your needs.

HOW DO I USE IT?

Fill out a Computer Search Request Form (available at the Circulation Desk). Just as in using a printed index, you will have a search statement . . . the topic of your thesis, research paper, report, speech, etc. From this you need to determine subjects pertinent to the topic along with synonyms, broader or narrower terms. Then consult with a librarian who can help refine your statement.

Rockford College
Howard Colman Library

5050 East State Street
Rockford, Illinois 61101

Actual size of document - 8½ x 5½ inches

HOW MUCH WILL IT COST?

The actual cost of your search will depend on the speed of the computer, the amount of information available on your topic, and the amount of thought you have given toward defining your subject. Each search is unique.

Searching by means of the computer is an alternative to manual searching of the indexes and there are some costs involved, such as royalty fees to the owners and long distance telephone charges. A nominal surcharge is also assessed. All fees are payable upon completion of the search.

SCHEDULING

Searches may be scheduled at the Circulation Desk. It is not absolutely necessary for you to be here when the search is done, but results may be better if you are present. A phone number is necessary in case the search requires personal choices because of terminology or costs.

INTERLIBRARY LOAN

Any items found by your search which are not available in our own collection can be requested through Inter-library Loan. Allow a minimum of 10 days for receipt of these items. There is no charge for this service.

GLOSSARY

Here are some terms you will be hearing as we talk about your computer-assisted reference search.

Abstract	A brief summary giving the essential content of an article.
Bibliographic	Information about sources you have used. Includes author, title, publisher and date of book, and title of magazine, date of issue, and page for magazine articles.
Citations	Lists of bibliographic descriptions.
Database	Index stored in a computer.
Hits	Number of times the computer finds information on your topic.
Offline Print	Printing done by computer after communications ends.
Search Statement	The topic of your report, paper, speech, etc.

TELEPHONE _____ (815) 226-4036

HOURS _____ Mon. — Fri.   9 a.m. - 4 p.m.

SEARCH REQUEST

FORMS/WORKSHEETS

CASTLETON STATE COLLEGE

Castleton, Vermont 05735 ● (802) 468-5611

LIBRARY

Database Search Request

Date _____

Name _____ Phone # _____

Mailing Address _____

Academic Department or Major _____

Faculty ( ) Administration ( ) Staff ( ) Undergraduate ( )

Graduate ( ) Other _____

1) Reason for search: Instruction ( )   Research ( )
                       Publication ( )   Other _____

2) Have you performed a manual search? _____ If so,
   which indexes or sources did you use?

   _____

   _____

3) In at least several sentences, describe the topic to be
   searched. Be as specific as possible.

   _____

   _____

   _____

   _____

4) Divide your search topic into major concepts or elements. For
   each concept, provide key words, thesaurus terms, synonyms,
   possible alternative spellings and phrasing used in the professional literature as related to your topic.

   Concept A _____

   Concept B _____

   Concept C _____

   Concept D _____

5) Please give a complete citation of at least one relevant article covering your topic.

_____

_____

_____

6) Are there any areas related to your search topic that you are NOT interested in ?

_____

_____

_____

7) Do you want document citations in a specific language ?

English only ( )   Other languages (list) _____

8) What specific time span would you like the search to cover? (Databases vary, but many begin their coverage as of 1966, some even earlier.)

_____

9) How many relevant citations do you expect a literature search will retrieve?

_____

10) Other helpful hints--Please give any information not specifi- cally asked for that may be helpful in conducting your search.

_____

_____

_____

****

***NOTE: Patrons requesting searches must discuss their search topic with one of CSC Library's database searches, Sandy Duling or Nancy Luzer. Searches generally can not be performed without this interview. Telephone: 468-5611, ext. 257

NEED HELP FILLING OUT THIS FORM? SEE A REFERENCE STAFF MEMBER!!!

DICKINSON COLLEGE LIBRARY
DATABASE SEARCH REQUEST

NAME: _____   DEPT./HUB BOX # _____

PHONE: _____   NEED RESULTS BY: _____

ARE YOU: Dickinson Student _____   Faculty/Acad. Prof. _____   Admin. _____

            Student at_____   Other_____

1. What is the topic you are researching? What type of project (e.g., term paper, research article) are you working on?

2. Have you used printed indexes (such as Reader's Guide or the MLA Bibliography)? If so, what subject terms have you found useful?

3. Are there any authors who have published important research on your topic, or are there authors whose work you wish to find?

4. If you can use literature in languages other than English, which languages?

5. Do you wish to limit the search to a time span, e.g., studies done since 1976? (Note that computerized databases are a fairly recent development; few include literature older than the mid-1970's.)

6. Would you prefer a broad search, retrieving more references, including many you can't use, or a narrow search, possibly missing relevant references?

LIBRARY USE ONLY
****

SEARCHER: _____   SYSTEM: _____   DATE: _____

EST. COST: _____   BILL PATRON/DEPT: _____   LIBRARY PAYMT: _____

43

Starr Library - Middlebury College

REQUESTING AN ONLINE DATABASE SEARCH
through
STARR LIBRARY, MIDDLEBURY COLLEGE

The Reference Department of Starr Library provides access to computer-readable
files through several vendors, including DIALOG Information Services, BRS
(Bibliographic Retrieval Services), and H.W. Wilson's Wilsonline. The service
is free to Middlebury College students, faculty, and staff working on course or
college-related projects.

Patrons desiring a search should provide complete information on this form and
bring it to the Reference Desk at Starr Library. A reference librarian will
need to interview you before planning a search strategy. The librarian will
make an appointment with you for the actual search. Your presence during the
online search greatly increases the accuracy of the results.

If you need help in filling out this request form, or have any questions
concerning online searching, please ask a reference librarian.

****

ONLINE SEARCH REQUEST FORM

Name:_____ Date:_____

Dept:_____ Status:_____ Phone:_____

Date by which search is needed:_____

A librarian will contact you to set up the appointment. What times are best for
you?_____

Purpose of search (Please circle.): term paper, teaching, research, thesis or
dissertation, or other (Please specify.)_____

****

1. Please give a title to your search.

_____

_____

2. Please give a narrative description of the problem to be searched. Be
   specific; define phrases with special meaning.

_____

_____

_____

_____

44

3. Please indicate key words or phrases which should be included in the search strategy and arrange them into concept groups. Within one concept group would be alternative ways of expressing the same idea--synonyms, variations in spelling, scientific or technical terms, or acronyms. The concepts will narrow or broaden the search when combined together.

concept 1   concept 2   concept 3

_____   _____   _____

_____   _____   _____

_____   _____   _____

_____   _____   _____

4. Are there any topics related to your specific problem that are <u>not</u> of interest? List below those you wish to <u>exclude</u>.

_____

_____

5. Please write down the complete citations, including author's full name, to two or three of the most useful articles on your search topic. (It may be helpful to bring these articles to your appointment.)

_____

_____

_____

6. Please list the titles of two or three of the most important journals covering your topic.

_____

_____

7. Please list the names of two or three of the most important authors publishing on your topic.

_____

_____

8. Can you use materials written in any language?_____   English only?_____
   English and _____

9. Do you wish to limit the search to a particular time span?_____
   If so, which years?_____

10. Have you manually searched any indexes?_____ If so, which titles and which years?

Dulaney-Browne Library
2501 N. Blackwelder
Oklahoma City, OK 73106

OKLAHOMA
CITY UNIVERSITY

ONLINE SEARCH REQUEST
(To be completed with the
assistance of a librarian)

SEARCH #_____
DATE REQUESTED_____
INTERVIEWER_____
SEARCHER_____
TIME ONLINE_____
ACTUAL COST_____
PATRON COST_____
DATE COMPLETED_____

NAME_____ TELE:_____
                                            (Home)   (Office)
FAC_____STAFF_____ GRAD. STUDENT _____ STUDENT LIBRARY CARD _____

TOPIC: Please describe your topic in sentence form as completely
and thoroughly as possible.

CONCEPTS: Break your topic down into 2 or 3 major concepts and list any
synonymns you can think of for each concept. It may be helpful to
consult a subject thesaurus or periodical index for terms. For
example:

    TOPIC: The relationship between stress and heart disease
           in the elderly.

CONCEPT I	CONCEPT II	CONCEPT III
stress	heart disease	elderly
SYNONYMS	**SYNONYMS**	**SYNONYMS**
anxiety	coronary disease	aged/aging
tension	cardiovascular disease	retirees
	cardiac disease	senior citizens

CONCEPT I	CONCEPT II	CONCEPT III
SYNONYMS	**SYNONYMS**	**SYNONYMS**

46

9-89

NOT WANTED: List concepts and related key words to be **EXCLUDED** from the search:

RELATED ARTICLES: List at least one article (author, title, journal) you have found that is relevant to your topic.

ABSTRACTS AND INDEXES: List abstracts, indexes or other paper sources you have consulted or feel would be productive to consult:

SEARCH LIMITATIONS:

Languages: _____ English only _____ Other languages (Please specify):

Years: _____ Entire database (some go back to the 1960s)

_____ Restrict search to (specify range of years): _____

Publication types (cross out types **not** wanted):
Periodicals   Books   Dissertations   Others (specify):

Number of citations/references needed:

_____ Minimum   _____ Maximum

Number of citations/references expected:

_____ Few (0-10)

_____ Lots (30-50)

NOTES: (Please note here any other information relating to your topic which will assist the searcher in this search.)

Howard Colman Library - Rockford College

Rockford College

Howard Colman Library
815/226-4035

ON-LINE SEARCH REQUEST FORM

5050 East State Street
Rockford, Illinois 61101

Patron:_____Date:_____

Address:_____Zip:_____

Telephone: (home)_____(office)_____

Status: Faculty_____Staff_____Graduate Student_____Undergraduate_____Other_____

Affiliation: R.C._____Other:_____

All information must be given before the search request will be processed.

SEARCH REQUEST: What subject do you want searched? Be as specific as possible.
Include synonyms and related terms. Note any material to be excluded from the search.

_____

_____

_____

_____

_____

_____

_____

Please Complete Reverse Side

Howard Colman Library - Rockford College

Do any of the items listed below suggest to you other information which might help us formulate a good comprehensive search? If so, please elaborate after each list.
Special terms: jargon, popular names (of laws, reports, etc.), abbreviations.

People and books: authors, persons associated with the subject, journal titles, book titles.

Organizations: conferences, associations, foundations, schools, institutes, government agencies, international organizations, congressional committees.

Commercial activities: industries, products, commodities.

Geographical areas: regions, countries, states, counties, cities, congressional districts.

Relevant citations: list important books or articles on the subject you have already found.

SEARCH LIMITS:

Would you prefer:

_____a comprehensive search that retrieves most of the references relevant to your topic but which may also retrieve many references not relevant? (Higher cost search)
                                    OR
_____a narrow search that may retrieve fewer references relevant to the topic but which also retrieves fewer non-relevant references: (Lower cost search)
Maximum number of citations desired:
_____1 - 25 _____26 - 50 _____51 - 100 _____All _____Other_____
                                                                    Specify
(If more than 100 citations are desired, they will be printed more economically at the computer facility and will be mailed within 5 - 10 days)
English language only_____ Other languages:_____
                                                        Specify

Years to be searched (e.g. 1978-82)_____Do you want a search update?____Yes____No.

Preferred print-out format: _____Citations only _____Abstracts (Useful but increases cost due to increased time on-line)

Bases:	Cost:	Acct. no.

Bases:_____   Cost:_____   Acct. no._____
       _____   _____   Make check payable to:
       _____   _____   Rockford College
       _____
                           Surcharge:_____   Mail to:
                                                        Howard Colman Library
                             TOTAL:_____   Rockford College
                                                        5050 E. State St.
                                    49   Rockford, Illinois 61101

Howard Colman Library - Rockford College

Rockford College

Howard Colman Library
815/226-4035

5050 East State Street
Rockford, Illinois 61101

MEMORANDUM

DATE:

  TO:

  RE: YOUR ON-LINE LITERATURE SEARCH

Your search was performed in the following database(s)_____

_____on_____.

_____   Your search may be picked up at the circulation desk. The search

         fee is _____.

_____   The citations that were printed on-line are attached. The rest of the
         citations are being printed more economically at the computer facility
         and will be mailed to us. You will be notified and billed when they
         arrive. Delivery time is usually 5-10 days.

_____   A problem was encountered in the processing of your search. Please

         contact _____(815) 226-4035 in the

         Howard Colman Library at your convenience.

Please note:_____

         _____

         _____

         _____

         _____

Please feel free to ask any questions you have concerning this search. We would be
happy to explain other services we have to offer such as our Current Awareness
Service which automatically searches the literature every month for a predetermined
set of queries.

                                        _____
                                        Search Analyst

INSTRUCTIONAL

MATERIALS/GUIDES

D I A L O G

Instructions for Using DIALOG
with the
Vectra and Dialoglink

----All keyboard executions are in "quotes"----

A. Choose **Dialog** from the PAM menu screen.(Use arrows to
   highlight choice). "Enter"

   1. Press any key.

B. Choose **Dialog** from Service Directory. "Enter"

C. You will be prompted to start **Accounting.**
   Choose yes(y).
   The Accounting form will appear where you should:

   1. Enter your subject in the **Subject** box.
   2. Enter your instructor's last name in the
      Client window.
   3. Enter your password in the **Searcher** window.
   4. Press "Enter" when complete.

D. The cursor block will appear on a black line at the
   bottom of the screen. This is where you will enter
   your search strategy.

1. Type "b" or "begin", and then the number of the
   database(s) you wish to search:

   "b55" "Enter"

   This command indicates you would like to search File or
   Database #55 which is <u>Biological Abstracts</u>. After
   typing the File#, press the enter key which moves you
   down a line for your next command.

   NOTE: You may search several databases at one time
   simply by listing their numbers in a string separated
   by commas:

   b55,34,434

D. On the next line you will type your search statement.

   ----All Search Statements Must Begin With "ss"----

1. Type "ss" and then the word(s) or phrase(s) that you
   wish to search:

   ss phytochrome and protein

In this statement you have asked for all
records(abstracts, etc.) of articles that include
both the word "phytochrome" and the word "protein."

NOTE: There are three logical operators for combining
words and/or phrases--**and, or,** and **not.**

OTHER EXAMPLES:

   ss exports and cash()crops

Always include "()" between words to indicate a phrase.
By editing this same method with a number, you may ask
for words in proximity in a record:

   ss exports and cash(3n)crops

This statement asks for records where the word
"cash" falls within 3 words either side of "crops" in
the text.

2. After you have completed your search statement,
   press "Enter".

3. If all terms look they way you intended, then it's
   time to go online. Press "f5" to connect online.
   Dialog will retrieve your search and display
   results like this:

S1	123108	EXPORTS
S2	1024	CASH
S3	786	CROPS
S4	102	CASH()CROPS
S5	41	EXPORTS AND CASH()CROPS

E. In order to display the 41 records or a portion of them
   you type a three-part command, each part separated by
   a backslash(/):

   "t5/5/1-20"

   t(type)**5**(set#)**/ 5**(code for full record)**/ 1-
   20**(number of records you want displayed.

To see all 41 records simply type "all" after the last "/".

The citations will scroll buy on the screen, but will be loaded in the "Retrieve Buffer"

!!!ALWAYS PRESS "F5" WHEN DONE WHETHER YOU PRINT OR NOT!!!

SAVING TO DISK

At any time you want to save your citations, abstracts, search strategy, or anything that appears on the screen, press the "F7" key. A menu will appear that, among other things, allows you to save a file to disk. Name the file, press enter and the file will be saved in order to be recalled later by using the same "F7" key and **loading** the saved file.

PRINTING CITATIONS
and
ABSTRACTS

I. Press "f5" to Logoff.

o

A. Use the"Pg Up" key to scroll back through the screens until you see the first citations, or records, that you would like to print. If the ones you want are close to the beginning of your session then you may use the "Home" key to carry you back to the very first.

1. Scroll the citations so that the first line you want to mark to be printed is positioned as the very bottom line on the screen.

2. Press "f4". The bottom line will be highlighted. Continue to scroll down(use "Pg Dn" or the arrow keys) through all lines you want marked for printing. At any point you want not to mark the citations press "f4" again. Press it again to begin marking.

3. When you have marked all the citations to be printed, press "f8".

4. Choose "2" (Print Retrieve Buffer Contents) from the menu.

5. Press "Enter". The "M" command for printing marked lines is the default.

6. Press simultaneously, "Ctrl", "Alt", and the "*" key next to the number pad on the far right of the keyboard to activate the printer in the lab.

- FOR ANY QUESTIONS ABOUT DIALOG OR THE ONLINE PROCEDURE -

- CALL STEVE RICHARDSON AT THE LIBRARY -----2192 or 2190 -

LaFayette College - David Bishop Skillman Library
BIOLOGY 101 LIBRARY PROJECT

In completing your Biology 101 library project, you may utilize Dialog, a computerized searching service which will allow you to search the Biological Abstracts database. A successful search consists of several related steps.

Before you sit down at the computer terminal, you will need to plan your search strategy.

1. Narrow the broad topic which you were given in class.

2. Check some of the paper indexes discussed during your class in the library. Note the keywords under which articles on your topic are indexed.

3. Write a brief statement of your search topic here:

_____

4. Select the two or three major concepts which best identify your topic and list them here: _____

_____

5. Look at each of the concepts which you have identified. Are there synonyms for one or more of the concepts? If you want to instruct the computer to look for either of two words in an article, you will type the first word, then type the word 'or' followed by the second word. The computer will find articles which include either the first word or the second word but not necessarily both words in the same article. You will want to use 'or' if some of your keywords are synonyms.

FOR EXAMPLE: If you are interested in the feeding habits of crocodiles, you might want to enter the part of the search dealing with feeding as: FEEDING OR EATING.

6. Are there any words in your search statement which have several possible endings? If you wish to enter a word which has several endings, any of which would be acceptable to you, type the root of the word followed by a question mark. This is known as truncating the word.

FOR EXAMPLE: Articles containing information about crocodiles may include the word 'crocodile' or the word 'crocodiles'. In order to retrieve articles which include both endings, enter the word as 'crocodile?'

7. List the two or three major concepts which identify your topic and their synonyms here. Truncate any terms which need to be truncated.

1. _____ OR _____

2. _____ OR _____

3. _____ OR _____

SAMPLE SEARCH STATEMENT

My topic is the feeding habits of crocodiles. In examining the print tools discussed in class, I have discovered that the words 'crocodile' or 'crocodiles' and 'feeding' occur in most of the articles. However, in some cases the word 'eating' is used instead of 'feeding'. Therefore, my keywords are: CROCODILE, CROCODILES, FEEDING and EATING.

In formulating my search statement, I truncate the word 'crocodile' by adding the question mark. This word will be entered into the computer as CROCODILE? and will retrieve articles including the words 'crocodile' and 'crocodiles.'

The part of the search statement which includes the words for feeding behavior must include both 'eating' and 'feeding' since either could be used in the articles which I wish to locate. Since the articles need to include at least one but not necessarily both of these terms, the part of the search statement containing the terms for feeding behavior would be entered as FEEDING OR EATING.

Since I need to locate articles which include the words CROCODILE? and FEEDING OR EATING, I would enter the search in the computer by typing: CROCODILE? when I am first asked for my subject. Dialog will then give me a list of several options including the option to narrow my search. I would press the n key to indicate that I wish to narrow my search. I would then type FEEDING OR EATING when the computer asks for the topic. By narrowing the search, I have told Dialog that I want only those articles which include the terms CROCODILE? and FEEDING OR EATING. I am now ready to have Dialog run the search against the computerized database of Biological Abstracts.

LaFayette College - David Bishop Skillman Library

CONDUCTING YOUR SEARCH

When you arrive for your search session, the Biology Project Assistant will review your search strategy with you and give you a password for Dialog.

SYSTEM ACTION	YOUR ACTION
1. C>(should be showing on screen)	2. Type: cd\xtalk[Return]
3. C>(will appear again)	4. Type: xtalk[Return]
5. A greeting screen then a menu will appear.	6. Type: 1[Return]
7. Telephone will be dialed and connected and the screen will go blank and an f` will appear.	8. Type: a
9. A three line message will appear with a colon at the end.	10. Type: dialog2[Return]
11. DIALOG INFORMATION SERVICES PLEASE LOGON:	12. Type: [Return]
13. ENTER PASSWORD:	14. Type password [Return]
15. You will now see the Dialog logon message and a ? at the beginning of the next line. Whenever Dialog expects you to type something, you will see a ?	16. Type: b dmc[Return]
17. Dialog will log in to the Dialog Medical Connection Main Menu which includes a list of 5 "libraries"	18. Type: 2[Return]
19. Dialog will respond with a list of eight databases.	20. Type: 2[Return]

59

21. Dialog will give you the option of searching by menu mode or by command mode.

22. Type: 1[Return]

23. Dialog will give you the option of searching by author or by subject.

24. You may search by either but most of you will wish to search by subject. Type: 1[Return]

25. Dialog will now ask you to enter terms describing one concept which you wish to search.

26. Enter the concept and its synonyms as instructed on the screen and press [Return].

27. You will now be given several options including the ability to narrow your search and to process the search.

28. Type: n[Return] to narrow your search and enter the second concept and its synonyms, if appropriate. Repeat the process until all search terms have been entered. Then press [Return] to process the search.

29. Dialog will process the search, indicate the number of records retrieved and give you the option of limiting your search.

30. You may limit the search by selecting one of the numbers and pressing [Return] or proceed without limiting by pressing [Return].

31. Dialog will now give you
    a list of options.

32. Type: 3[Return]

33. Dialog will now give you a
    list of display options.

34. Type: 1[Return]
    Press the F6 key

35. Dialog will now ask how many
    references you wish to display.

36. Please display no more
    than 25 at a time.

37. Dialog will return to the
    display menu.

38. When you have finished
    printing or when your
    time is up, type: /1
    [Return].

39. You will be logged off the
    system.

40. Press the escape key
    and type: quit[Return]

41. C> will reappear

42. Please enter your
    search in the log.

TRANSACTION LOG FORMS

St. John's University - Alcuin Library

ONLINE DATABASE SEARCH

LOG SHEET

Date	Srchr	Patron Status	Search Topic	Vendor	File	#Types/ Prints	Time Online	Signoff Time	Actual Cost	Patron Cost
									$	$
									$	$
									$	$
									$	$
									$	$
									$	$
									$	$
									$	$
									$	$
									$	$
									$	$
									$	$
									$	$
									$	$
									$	$
									$	$

Margaret Clapp Library - Wellesley College

LOCATION: _____ CLAPP LIBRARY: MEDIATED COMPUTER SEARCHING
MAY 1 _____ to APRIL 30 _____

	DIALOG	WILSONLINE	EPIC	RLIN	TOTAL
Reference student					
Reference faculty					
Reference staff					
SUBTOTAL					
Extended student					
Extended faculty					
Extended staff					
SUBTOTAL					
TOTALS					

c:\wp5\wpdocs\searchst.fom

BILLING FORMS

Albright College

COMPUTERIZED LITERATURE SEARCH SERVICE

INVOICE No. _____

To: _____   Date: _____

_____

Data Base _____
    Connect time: _____ hours   @ $ /hr. $
    Online type charges: _____ types @ $ /each $
    Offline print charges: _____ prints @ $ $

Data Base _____
    Connect time: _____ hours   @ $ /hr $
    Online type charges: _____ types @ $ /each $
    Offline print charges: _____ prints @ $ $

Data Base _____
    Connect time: _____ hours   @ $ /hr $
    Online type charges: _____ types @ $ /each $
    Offline print charges: _____ prints @ $ $

Data Base _____
    Connect time: _____ hours   @ $ /hr $
    Online type charges: _____ types @ $ /each $
    Offline print charges: _____ prints @ $ $

                 Telecommunications $
                 Fees $_____
                 TOTAL COST $

Please make all checks payable to Albright College Library. Address all corresepondence to Rosemary Deegan, c/o Albright College Library, P.O. Box 15234, Reading, PA 19612-5234.

69

AURORA UNIVERSITY
COMPUTERIZED REFERENCE SERVICE
Search Request

Name:		Search Number:		Date Searched:

Patron Status: Undergraduate_____ Graduate_____ Faculty____ Staff____ Other____

Address (Local):		Zip Code	Phone # (Home) Phone # (Work)

I hereby authorize AURORA UNIVERSITY LIBRARY to produce the online search(es) specified, and I agree to pay the charges incurred, even if the search results in no relevant citations. I understand that failure to pay can result in legal action (e.g., transcript, registration, or diploma holds) by the university.

X _____ Today's Date_____

The MAXIMUM AMOUNT OF MONEY I want to spend for this search is $_____

FULL PAYMENT IS REQUIRED AT THE TIME THE SEARCH RESULTS ARE RECEIVED.

SEARCH COSTS are generated by a combination of the following: (1) connect time, i.e., the amount of time a user is linked to the computer; (2) royalties, i.e., fees paid to the holder of the database copyright; (3) print charges, i.e., costs for printing and delivering resultant citations; and (4) communication costs, i.e., telephone charges from here to a computer network.

Databases Searched	File Number	Elapsed Time	Rate	Cost of Time	Cost of Prints	# of Prints	Total Cost
			$	$	$		$

Remarks:

SUBTOTAL .
Service Charge $ 1.00
TOTAL AMOUNT OWED

Searcher_____   Date Prints Rec'd_____   Date Patron Contacted_____
Date Paid or Billed _____: Cash_____ Check_____ Charge to Dept Acct #_____
Bill sent to LS _____   CREDIT ACCOUNT # _____

PLEASE LIST STATEMENT OF PROBLEM ON REVERSE SIDE OF THIS SHEET

072088:RAB

70

```
Communications  =======================================================

                    DIALOG SEARCH SESSION INVOICE

========================================================================


   Subject:          AV-Online Pre-Search
   Client Name:
   Charge Code:      Library
   Searcher:
   Date:             May 29, 1991
   Job No.:

--------------------------------------------------------------------------


   15:29
   DIALOG FILE 1
         Connect          $     0.12
         Types                  0.00
         Prints                 0.00
         Print Credits          0.00
         Reports                0.00
         Communications         0.04
                              ---------
         Total:           $     0.16     Connect Hours:  0.004

   15:29
   DIALOG FILE 46
         Connect          $     1.15
         Types                  0.15
         Prints                 0.00
         Print Credits          0.00
         Reports                0.00
         Communications         0.16
                              ---------
         Total:           $     1.46     Connect Hours:  0.016
--------------------------------------------------------------------------

   Total Session Cost:   $    1.62
   Total Connect Hours:       0.020
```

GEORGIA COLLEGE

WELLESLEY COLLEGE LIBRARY * * ONLINE SEARCH SERVICE * * # _____

Name _____

Student course _____
Faculty dept. _____
Staff dept. _____

DATE	DATABASE VENDOR	DATABASE	CONNECT TIME CHARGE	OFFLINE PRINT CHARGE	TOTAL
TOTAL					

Searcher _____

Date Invoice sent _____

Date paid _____

MINUS AMOUNT PAID BY LIBRARY	
AMOUNT TO BE PAID BY USER	

Paid by: ☐ Cash   ☐ Check   Budget No. _____

(Make checks payable to: Wellesley College)

This is a 3-part pressure-sensitive form measuring 8½ x 6¼ inches

EVALUATION FORMS

REDEEMER COLLEGE LIBRARY

Computer Search Evaluation Form

Name: _____ Date: _____

Subject of search: _____
Database(s): _____

****

1. Have you requested a computer search before? Yes ____ No ____

2. Was the purpose of this search to determine that no previous
    work had been done on this topic? Yes ____ No ____

3. Did this search provide enough <u>relevant</u> citations for the
    purpose for which you submitted the search request?
    Yes ____
    No, but I didn't expect to see anything ____
    No (please comment) _____
    _____

4. What percentage of the total citations provided by this
    search appears <u>relevant</u> to the specific question or topic
    for which you submitted a search request?

    0% ____   1-25% ____   26-50% ____   51-75% ____   76-100% ____

5. What percentage of the total citations provided by this
    search appears relevant to your <u>overall</u> information need,
    rather than simply to the specific search topic?

    0% ____   1-25% ____   26-50% ____   51-75% ____   76-100% ____

6. What percentage of the <u>relevant</u> citations are new to you?

    0% ____   1-25% ____   26-50% ____   51-75% ____   76-100% ____

7. Are the search results worth the cost you paid for the
    search? Yes ____ No (please comment) _____
    _____

8. Would you request a computer search again? Yes ____
    No (please comment) _____

9. Would you recommend this service to others? Yes ____
    No (please comment) _____

Additional Comments:

90/01/mn

Howard Colman Library - Rockford College

Rockford College

Howard Colman Library
815/226-4035

COMPUTER SEARCH EVALUATION

5050 East State Street
Rockford, Illinois
61108-2393

Please help us by rating our computerized literature search service as follows.
You may leave the form at the Circulation Desk or return it by mail. Thank you.

Status: Faculty_____Staff_____Graduate Student_____Undergraduate_____Other_____

Affiliation: R.C._____Other: _____

Please rate your search on a scale from zero to ten.   PLEASE CIRCLE ONE

1. How pleased are you with the search?   0 1 2 3 4 5 6 7 8 9 10
                                             very unhappy   very pleased

2. How useful are the results?   0 1 2 3 4 5 6 7 8 9 10
                                             useless   of great use

3. Are the citations reasonably   0 1 2 3 4 5 6 7 8 9 10
    relevant to your needs?   irrelevant   on target

4. Do you feel that the search was   0 1 2 3 4 5 6 7 8 9 10
    comprehensive?   too limited   covered all bases

5. Are the results in a useful format?   0 1 2 3 4 5 6 7 8 9 10
                                             useless   very useful

6. Did you receive the printout(s)   0 1 2 3 4 5 6 7 8 9 10
    quickly enough?   too slowly   timely

7. Do you feel that the librarian   0 1 2 3 4 5 6 7 8 9 10
    who took the request understood it?   not at all   completely

8. Would you use the service again if   0 1 2 3 4 5 6 7 8 9 10
    you needed literature research?   never   always

9. Do you feel the charge was   0 1 2 3 4 5 6 7 8 9 10
    reasonable?   too expensive   good value

10. How well did the results of the   0 1 2 3 4 5 6 7 8 9 10
    search meet your expectations of
    computerized literature searching?   very little   fully met

Transylvania University Library

DIALOG SEARCH EVALUATION FORM

Please take a few minutes to answer these questions regarding your
DIALOG search. The form is pre-addressed, so just fill it in and drop
it in the Transylvania Campus Mail or return it to the Circulation
Desk in the Transylvania Library.

1. Your name (optional)_____

2. Topic of your search_____

3. Date of your search_____

4. What was the product of your search?

        _____statistical data
        _____bibliography

If your answer to question 4 was statistical data, please answer only
items 7 and 8 on this form. If your answer was bibliography, please
answer all the remaining items on this form.

5. How many citations did you receive?

        _____5 - 10
        _____11 - 25
        _____over 25

6. How many of the citations were relevant?

        _____all
        _____75%
        _____50%
        _____25%
        _____none

7. Was your search successful?

        _____yes
        _____no

8. If not, why was it unsuccessful?

        _____you did not communicate the problem clearly to the searcher
        _____the searcher misunderstood the problem
        _____the searcher was unfamiliar with the DIALOG system
        _____there was no material on the subject

Comments_____

_____

Thank you.

CD-ROM DOCUMENTS

POLICY STATEMENTS

CD-ROM
POLICIES AND PROCEDURES

I. Acquisitions
    A. Criteria
       1. Quality of product/reputation of vendor
       2. Compatibility with acquired CD-ROM products re:
          hardware and command language
       3. Relevance of subject content to curriculum
       4. Scholarliness of product
       5. Price
    B. Budget
       1. Requests will include the following: hardware,
          software, documentation, furniture (two-tiered
          table, surge protector, security devices, chair),
          and supplies (paper, ink cartridges, disc
          cleaner)
       2. Budget division
          a) hardware: database searching
          b) CD-ROM subscription: acquisitions
          c) furniture: database searching
          d) security locks: database searching
          e) supplies:

II. Cataloging
    A. All CD-ROMs and any support materials intended for
       public use will be cataloged.

III. Physical set-up
    A. Environmental considerations
       1. Adequate wiring, lighting
       2. Room for cabling equipment together if necessary
       3. Close to Reference Desk
    B. Workstations
       1. In addition to hardware, each workstation should
          contain: documentation, sign-up sheet,
          appropriate thesauri, appropriate journal lists
    C. Supplies and Hardware and Software Documentation
       1. Ink-jet cartridges (on CD-ROM shelf)
       2. Disc cleaner (on CD-ROM shelf)
       3. All vendor documentation (on CD-ROM shelf)
       4. Archival discs (in CD-ROM drawer)
       5. Sign-up sheets (in CD-ROM drawer)
       6. Paper (one box in office, reserves in Room 135)
       7. System set-up diskettes (on CD-ROM shelf)
    D. Security
       1. Philips CD player (PsycLit)
          a) keys: two keys kept in "key drawer"
          b) cable lock combination:
       2. Hitachi CD player (Wilsondisc)
          a) no keys
          b) cable lock combination:
       3. Toshiba CD player (PAIS and BA)
          a) no keys

not sign up for more than 30 minutes.
D. Reserved time on the workstation will be
forfeited if the user does not show up within
10 minutes of his/her appointed time and someone
else wishes to use the system.
E. Reference librarians will not reserve time on the
workstation over the phone.
F. Patrons should be encouraged to print in the citation
(or citation-abstract) format and to print only those
records relevant to their research.

V.   User Aids and Instruction
A. Tutorial provided by system
B. Manual provided by system
C. Ready-reference guide devised by librarians
D. Notification sent to appropriate faculty
E. Notification sent to department majors along with an
invitation to sign up for a CD-ROM tutorial
F. BI sessions as appropriate

cdpolicy
rev. 10/90

b) cable lock combination:

E. Maintenance

1. CD-ROM workstations will be turned off when the Library closes. This will be done by the janitor responsible for closing the Library.

2. The first person on the desk will be responsible for turning on the workstation(s).

3. Discs will be cleaned on a weekly basis by the first person on Monday mornings.

4. All librarians will be responsible for fixing paper jams, loading paper, changing discs, and inserting new ink cartridges as the need arises. The printer manual should be consulted for instructions on how to operate and maintain the printer.

5. Supplies will be ordered by the Database Searching Coordinator. Librarians should notify the Coordinator when supplies of paper, ink cartridges, etc., are low.

6. Problems with either hardware or software not addressed in the troubleshooting section of this manual should be reported in detail to the Database Searching Coordinator, who will send a work form to Administrative Computing. In cases where the Coordinator is unavailable for an extended period of time, someone should take the responsibility of filling out a work form (kept in the white computer notebook by the IBM PC XT in the Reference Office) and sending it over to Administrative Computing. A copy of the work form should be kept for reference.

7. The Database Searching Coordinator will be responsible for making arrangements with Administrative Computing for installation of new equipment and software, and also for the upgrading of any component of the CD-ROM workstation.

IV. Access and Use

A. CDs may be utilized by anyone possessing a valid Vassar ID during the academic year and by any patron during the summer and other academic intercessions. Vassar Library will not honor Southeastern cards for the use of CD-ROMs when the patron's library already possesses the print version of that title.

B. Users may sign up for a maximum of 30 minutes. If at the end of their slot no one wishes to use the workstation, they may sign in for additional time until such time that another user wishes to use the workstation.

C. On Mondays, the first librarian on the desk will post a sign-up sheet at each workstation for the purposes of signing up in advance to reserve time. Users must

PROMOTIONAL LITERATURE

Drew University Library

INDEXES ON CD—ROM

WHAT ARE INDEXES ON CD—ROM?

Many indexes, previously available only in book form, are now published on a compact disc so they may be searched with the assistance of a computer.

WHAT IS THE ADVANTAGE OF SEARCHING ON A CD—ROM?

Because the computer is capable of looking for words anywhere in the bibliographic citation, more complex and more refined searches may be done. Combinations of terms that would be very tedious to search in the print version can be searched easily with the assistance of the computer.

WHAT INDEXES ARE AVAILABLE ON CD—ROM AT DREW?

GPO on Silver Platter — Corresponds to the Monthly Catalog of United States Government Publications. (1976+)

PsycLIT — Corresponds to Psychological Abstracts, an international index to journal articles, conference proceedings and dissertations in psychology and related fields. (1972+)

sociofile — Includes Sociological Abstracts, an international index to journal articles, conference proceedings and dissertations in sociology and related fields (1974+) and Social Planning/Policy and Development Abstracts (SOPODA) (1979+)

PAIS on CD—ROM — Corresponds to PAIS, an index covering books, journal articles, government publications, conference proceedings and reports dealing with social issues and public policy. (1972+)

Dissertation Abstracts Ondisc — Corresponds to Dissertation Abstracts listing and indexing Doctoral dissertations completed at most North American universities; recently selectively includes North American Masters theses and doctoral dissertations at certain European universities. (1861+) (only entries since 1980 contain abstracts)

Humanities Index — Corresponds to Humanities Index, an index in fields such as archaeology, classics, film, art, philosophy, world history and world literature. (1984+)

MLA International Bibliography — Corresponds to the MLA International Bibliography, an index of various books and periodicals in the field of modern language and literature. (1981+)

Religion Index - Corresponds to Religion Index One and Two, Index to Book Reviews in Religion, and Research in Ministry, indexes to international scholarly and denominational journals, essays, Festschriften and dissertations. (1975+)

Social Sciences Index - Corresponds to Social Sciences Index, an index to journal articles in fields such as anthropology, ethnic studies, international relations, political science, psychology, public administration, sociology, and urban studies. (1983+)

HOW DO I USE A CD-ROM?

All of the indexes, with the exception of GPO on Silver Platter, are kept at the Reserve Counter and must be checked out with a Drew ID card or some other form of identification. GPO is kept permanently in Workstation #1. PsycLIT, sociofile, PAIS, MLA Bibliography, and Dissertation Abstracts may be used on Workstations #2 and #3, near the Index Table, and #5 in the Microform Room. Humanities Index, MLA International Bibliography, Religion Index, and Social Sciences Index may be used only on Workstation #4.

Instructions for starting up the appropriate CD-ROMs are at each workstation. BE SURE TO FOLLOW THE INSTRUCTIONS FOR THAT INDEX AND THAT WORKSTATION. The indexes themselves have help available both on-screen and with manuals that are housed at the Reference Counter. In addition, there are one-page information sheets for each index at an information stand adjacent to the Reference Counter. The staff member on duty at the Reference Counter also is ready to assist you with either the technology or the search strategy.

Eastern Oregon State College

CD-ROM LAB
Walter M. Pierce Library
Eastern Oregon State College

Databases Available

AGRICOLA   1979-   3 disks   National Agricultural Library
International in scope, covers virtually every major agricultural subject in a database totalling
over 1.3 million citations. Spans a variety of publication including books, journals, dissertations,
technical reports, newspapers, manuscripts and data files. Audio-visual materials such as
filmstrips, slides, recordings, and maps are also indexed.

Agricultural Library   pre-1900-   1 disk   OCLC Online Union Catalog
Containing over 300,000 citations drawn from the OCLC Online Union Catalog (comprises over
19 million records). Virtually every type of publication is represented, from books, journals and
manuscripts to videotapes and microforms, gathered from domestic and foreign sources.

Agricultural/Retail Census   1988   1 disk   Bureau of the Census
Statistical data from the Census of Agriculture, 1982 and the Census of Retail Trade, 1982.

Books in Print Plus   Current year   1 disk   Bowker Publishing
Lists over 840,000 titles with bibliographic information which are currently in print. Also includes
complete names and addresses of book publishers.

Business Periodical Index   July, 1982-   1 disk   H.W. Wilson Co.
Indexes 345 of today's leading business journals. Subject coverage in accounting, acquisitions &
mergers, advertising, banking, economics, personnel, small business and many other related
areas.

CASSIS/CD-ROM   pre-1900-   3 disks   Patents and Trademarks Office
Indexes a patent search file which is one of the largest collections of technological literature in the
world. This file contains 13.8 million U.S. patent documents which are distributed among
114,000 classifications of technology.

County & City Data Book   1988   1 disk   Bureau of the Census
Includes demographic, governmental and economic data using the 1980 census and more recent
reports compiled by the other Federal and private agencies.

CRIS   Current   1 disk   U.S. Department of Agriculture
A computer-based documentation and reporting system for ongoing agricultural and forestry
research. Every quarter it provides a newly updated listing of over 30,000 abstracts and progress
reports for active and recently completed research in agriculture and related sciences.

issued 9/90

Economic Census   1913-   2 disks   Bureau of the Census
Statistical data compiled from eight databases including Consumer Price Index, Producer Price Index, Export-Import Index.

Educational Library   pre-1900-   1 disk   OCLC Online Union Catalog
Consists of 500,000 bibliographic records pertaining to education. All formats and types of materials are represented, including books , journals, theses, data files, computer programs, slides, newspapers, recordings, filmstrips, microforms, and manuscripts.

Environment Library   pre-1900-   1 disk   OCLC Online Union Catalog
Consists of bibliographic records pertaining to environmental sciences. All formats and types of materials are represented, including books , journals, theses, data files, computer programs, slides, newspapers, recordings, filmstrips, microforms, and manuscripts.

ERIC   1966-   3 disks   Educational Resources Information Center
The most complete bibliography of educational materials available. Drawn from over 400,000 citations listed in the Resources in Eduction and Current Index to Journals in Education indexes published and unpublished sources on thousands of educational topics.

General Science Index   May, 1984-   1 disk   H.W. Wilson Co.
Indexes current information in 109 english-language science journals. Subject coverage includes astronomy, atmospheric science, biology botany, chemistry, earth science, mathematics, physics, zoology and many more related disciplines.

GPO Monthly Catalog   July, 1976-   1 disk   U.S. Government Printing Office
Comprised of over 285,000 records, includes references to reports and hearings of Congressional committees, Congressional debates and records, reports of decisions by the Supreme Court and other federal courts, and documents issued y executive departments. Materials listed in the database include monographs, serials, statistics, maps, and reports.

Humanities Index   February, 1984-   1 disk   H.W. Wilson Co.
Indexes 345 english-language journals with subject coverage in art, archaeology, classical studies, dance, drama, journalism, language & literature, music, philosophy, and religion.

InfoTrac/Academic Index   Current 4 yrs 1 disk   Information Access Co.
Designed for research in the Humanities, Social Sciences, General Sciences, and current events. Provides bibliographic references to over 390 scholarly and general-interest journals, as well as six months coverage of the New York Times.

MLA International Bibliography   January, 1981-   1 disk   H.W. Wilson Co.
The largest and most comprehensive database covering current scholarship in the modern languages, literature, and folklore. The materials indexed include worldwide coverage from approximately 3,000 journals and monographs.

PsychLit   1974-   2 disks   American Psychological Association
Citations and abstracts of international journal articles in psychology and related disciplines. Covers over 1,400 journals, representing professional and scientific literature from over 50 countries.

Social Sciences Index   1983-   1 disk   H.W. Wilson Co.
Citations to articles and book reviews in over 300 English-language journals in the social sciences. Covers anthropology, economics, environmental sciences, law, planning and public administration, political science and many other related disciplines.

CD-ROM REMOTE ACCESS FOR THE DISTANT LEARNER

This project was designed to provide academic support to the distant learner through dial-in remote access to a CD-ROM search system which is housed at Eastern Oregon State College library. The project was funded through the U.S. Department of Education, College Library Technology and Cooperation Grants program and demonstrates that: 1) students attending small rural colleges and placebound students living in communities distant from campuses can have immediate and affordable access to information required for their studies and, 2) support of faculty teaching and research efforts at a small college is enhanced through improved access to information and data.

The mission statement for Eastern Oregon State College directs we serve the eastern-most ten counties of Oregon -- 42,000 square miles with only five communities having a population of more than 10,000 and none having a population over 15,000; the area accounts for 46% of Oregon's land mass but only 6% of the State's population. The project makes possible improved information access to college students and 140,000 residents in this region. In a rural area such as the one served it is very difficult to obtain scholarly material to provide academic support for the distant learner. During any one term approximately twenty-five percent of Eastern's enrollment (approximately 700 students) is comprised of students who are attending classes part-time at one of the regional outreach centers or on the main campus. These individuals tend to be placebound, work full-time and have family responsibilities distant from La Grande -- some as far as 300 miles -- delivery of support services, especially library support, has been a primary concern and the major reason for developing the CD-ROM search system. Before the implementation of the CD-ROM search system these students and patrons were reliant on information from their local small public libraries which were often inadequate to serve the academic needs of college students.

The distant learner in the ten county region may access the system via their own home personal computer and modem or at one of the sites in the area which has equipment available for use. The system does not require special software to search the databases other than the typical telecommunications package to connect to the search system. The student dials into the system on a toll-free line and then selects the appropriate responses on the main menu screen. There are fourteen databases currently available on the CD-ROM search system; once a file is chosen the student may begin the search process. The files cover subject matter in many different areas such as agriculture, education, sociology, linguistics, business and many others. When the student searches the system on a specific topic a bibliography of journal articles, book citations, and other relevant material is produced.

The CD-ROM search system is just one facet of a larger information system, the Eastern Oregon Information Network (EOIN), which was developed in 1987. The EOIN started as an electronic mail system with three very defined subsystems; 1) messaging, 2) interlibrary loan and, 3) an online serials holdings list of the largest libraries in the group of 109 participants. In 1989, with the Department of Education grant award, the EOIN was expanded to include online information retrieval through CD-ROM technology. By linking the Eastern Oregon Information Network with the CD-ROM search system, this allowed the student to dial into the search system and find bibliographic citations to satisfy research needs then place an interlibrary loan to retrieve the material through the same system.

The concept of fully utilizing CD-ROM technology through a dial-access multi-user, multi-access system has been discussed before but the available technology would not support the idea. Eastern Oregon State College custom developed a system based on the UNIX operating system to provide the first remote access, multi-user, multi-access CD-ROM search system.

8th & K, La Grande, OR 97850
(503)963-2171 — Toll free in Oregon 1-800-452-8639
A Member of the Oregon State System of Higher Education

Julia Rogers Library
Goucher College

CD-ROM SEARCHING OPTIONS

JOURNAL AND NEWSPAPER INDEXES

1.   **INFOTRAC: Academic Index (Lobby)**

Indexes editorial and news magazines; scholarly journals from the humanities, sciences, and social sciences; and recent issues of the New York Times. Covers the last 4 years of popular journals, past 6 months of New York Times, and research journals from 1/87 or 1/89. Updated monthly during the school year. Find citations to articles by subject, author, or name.

2.   **INFOTRAC: National Newspaper Index (Lobby)**

Indexes the New York Times, Wall Street Journal, Washington Post, Christian Science Monitor, and Los Angeles Times for the past 4 years. Updated monthly. Library subscribes to 4 of the 5 newspapers (no LA Times). Find citations to articles by subject or name.

3.   **WILSONDISC: General Science Index (Lobby)**

Indexes journals in the areas of biological sciences, environment, chemistry, physics, medicine, nutrition, genetics, mathematics, astronomy. Coverage begins 5/84. Searchable by subject, author, name, journal, key words. Online access for most recent citations. To find citations to earlier articles, use the printed form of the General Science Index. (Index Table)

4.   **WILSONDISC: Humanities Index (Lobby)**

Indexes journals in the areas of literature, history, film, music, communications, philosophy and religion. Searchable by subject, author, name, journal, key words. Coverage begins 2/84. Online access for most recent citations. To find citations to earlier articles, use the printed form of the Humanities Index. (Index Table)

5.   **WILSONDISC: MLA International Bibliography**

Indexes journals, series, monographs, working papers, conference papers and proceedings, bibliographies, catalogs, handbooks, dictionaries and other types of reference works in the areas of literature, language, linguistics and folklore. Searchable by subject, author, name and journal or book title. Coverage begins in 1981. This file corresponds to the print version of the MLA International Bibliography of Books and Articles on the Modern Languages and Literatures. (Ref 800Q M689m)

6.   **WILSONDISC: Social Sciences Index (Lobby)**

Indexes journals in the areas of economics, international relations, psychology, politics, sociology, and anthropology. Searchable by subject, author, name, journal, key words. Coverage begins 2/83. Online access for most recent citations. To find citations to earlier articles, use the printed form of the Social Sciences Index. (Index Table)

FULL TEXT ENCYCLOPEDIA

7. Electronic Encyclopedia (Lobby)

CD-ROM form of the 1988 Academic American Encyclopedia. Search by name, subject, or key words. Can print out paragraphs or whole articles. Can save information to floppy disk.

UNION CATALOG OF BOOKS

8. MICROCAT: OLDCAT and NEWCAT (Lobby)

Citations to some books, journals, and audio-visual materials available in Maryland public and academic libraries. You will still need to check the card catalog if you want a complete list of Goucher Library holdings. Access by author, title, and keyword. Updated annually. Is six months to 2 years out-of-date.

BOOKS IN PRINT AND REVIEWS

9. Books in Print PLUS with Reviews (Online Office)

Citations to books in print, recently out of print, and books to be printed in the near future. Search by author, title, subject, key words, publisher, etc. More recently published book citations also include full text reviews from journals such as Booklist, Publisher's Weekly, and Library Journal. Updated quarterly. Appointment and some instruction are needed to search.

BIBLIOGRAPHY OF FEDERAL DOCUMENTS

10. MARCIVE GPO/CAT PAC (Lobby)

Indexes U.S. government documents from July 1976 to the present. Searchable by title, keywords, subject, author and document number. Updated quarterly. Use the Monthly Catalog of U.S. Government Publications to find documents published earlier.

8/90

INSTRUCTIONAL

MATERIALS/GUIDES

INFOTRAC DATABASE

InfoTrac contains references to articles from approximately 1100 journals covering business, management, and general interest. References from the current year plus the three previous years are included (1985 to present). The database contains references from the last six months of the *Wall Street Journal* and the last 60 days of the *New York Times*. InfoTrac is updated monthly.

HOW TO SEARCH

References or citations are arranged under an alphabetical listing of subject headings, corporate or personal names and titles of books, movies, etc., about which articles have been written. Under the individual subject headings, the references are further organized by various sub-headings. For additional assistance, many of the subject headings are followed by a display of related subjects (SEE or SEE ALSO references).

SAMPLE JOURNAL CITATION

TAX SHELTERS <--[subject heading]
  see also
    COMMODITY TAX STRADDLES <---------------------------------------[related heading]
    SAFE HARBOR LEASING
  -ACCOUNTING <--[subheading]
    Funds that cut your taxes. Changing Times-Nov '85 p96(2) <---------------------[reference]
     | | | |
   Article title   Journal title Publication Date Beginning page number & no. of succeeding pages

SAMPLE NEWSPAPER CITATION

TAX SHELTERS
  -ANALYSIS
  = Finding tax shelter in a second home. by Deborah Rankin il New York Times v136 Jan 18, '87 sec 3
   pF11(N) pF11(L) col 1

In the newspaper citations, the *New York Times* uses N and L with the pages to indicate the National or Late edition. Albright subscribes to the Late edition. For the *Wall Street Journal*, E or W are used with the page numbers to indicate the Eastern or Western edition. Albright subscribes to the Eastern edition

HOW TO ENTER TOPIC

Here are some examples of how to enter your topic:

Personal Names	*Company Names*	*Subjects*
Adams, John Quincy	General Motors Corp	Tax credits
Adams	General Motors	Brown v. Allen
Adams, John	Toyota	Clean Air Act
Adams, J	Toyota Celica	New York City

After entering your search topic, press the SEARCH/ENTER key. If several subheadings appear under your search topic, you will be requested to enter a subheading. Press the SEARCH key to bypass this option, or enter a subheading and then press SEARCH. *EXACT MATCH:* When there is an exact match for you subject, InfoTrac will take you directly to the display of the first citation. You may browse the data by using the movement keys (NEXT LINE or PRIOR LINE) or print a reference by pressing the PRINT REF key. If you do not wish to browse the citations, return to the thesaurus of subjects and subject headings by pressing the SUBJECT GUIDE key. *NO MATCH:* If no exact match is found, you will be shown the alphabetical subject listing at the point most closely matching your topic. Use the movement keys to browse the SUBJECT GUIDE of headings and subheadings. Once you find a heading or a cross reference of interest, position the pointer at the desired term and press the SEARCH/ENTER key. When doing a search involving one or more SEE ALSO references, use the BackTrac key if you wish to return to a previous topic. *CHANGING TOPICS:* To begin a new search, press START/FINISH. If you have printed any citations, this will eject the paper enough for you to tear it off the printer. To make tearing the paper easier, please hold the printer cover down while tearing. *NEED HELP:* Ask at the Reference Desk.

WHAT IS INFOTRAC?

InfoTrac is an automated reference system that allows you to retrieve bibliographic references (citations) stored on compact disc (CD ROM).

The InfoTrac system is designed specifically for public access. YOU DO NOT NEED A MANUAL OR SPECIAL TRAINING TO USE THE SYSTEM. Each search step is self-explanatory, and the color-coded function keys on the keyboard allow you to retrieve, display, and print article references.

The data card attached to the unit also describes the function of each color-coded key. You can get more detailed information by pressing the HELP key at any point during a search.

The database available in our libraries is the *Academic Index*. It is designed for research in the Humanities, Social Sciences, General Sciences, and Current Events. It provides bibliographic references (citations) to over 390 scholarly and general interest periodicals, as well as 6 months coverage of the *New York Times*. It covers the most current 3-4 years of information and is updated monthly.

HOW THE INFORMATION IS ORGANIZED

InfoTrac uses *Library of Congress Subject Headings* (LCSH) with additional headings for new and topical subjects. Headings may be topics; personal (last name first), corporate or product names; titles of books, movies, plays, etc.

References are arranged alphabetically and appear in reverse chronological order under each heading or subheading. Each reference indicates the number of pages in the article, as well as bibliographical details such as author, title of article, periodical title, and date.

HOW TO SEARCH

After entering your topic, press the SEARCH/ENTER (return) key. When there is an exact match in the subject listing for the entered topic, InfoTrac will take you directly to the SUBJECT GUIDE which shows you the full listing of headings and subheadings, as well as cross-references ("SEE" and "SEE ALSO").

To view the citations under any heading, position the cursor (highlighted line) at the term by using the NEXT LINE/PRIOR LINE keys and press the SEARCH/ENTER (return) key. Another screen, a citations window, will display the bibliographic references under that heading. You can print the references in the citations window by using the PRINT key.

Position the pointer at the SEE or SEE ALSO heading and press the SEARCH/ENTER (return) key if you wish to search these cross-referenced terms. To return to the SUBJECT GUIDE, press the left arrow key.

If no exact match is found for the topic you have entered, you will be shown the alphabetical subject listing that best matches your topic. You can browse the alternate headings by using the NEXT LINE/PRIOR LINE keys, or you can start a new search by pressing the START/FINISH key.

HINTS
or items that do not easily fit in elsewhere in this guide

The six letter/number code that may appear at the end of an entry refers to a free text microfilm magazine collection. The libraries do **NOT** have this collection, so you can safely, but unhappily, ignore this bit of data.

The letters (N) or (L) following a page number in a *New York Times* citation refer to the National Edition and the Late Edition of that newspaper. **Use the L (Late) citation.**

The letters (W) or (E) following a page number in a *Wall Street Journal* citation indicate the Western or Eastern edition. **Use the E (Eastern) citation.**

In reviews of books, movies, restaurants, plays, etc. a letter code grading system (A, best - F, worst) gives you a general idea of the reviewer's opinion.

Each time you use the **BACKTRAC** key you will move back one step in your search process. This is especially useful when you are searching a topic that has many SEE ALSO references.

If you want to find out if a certain periodical is indexed by *Academic Index*, type **LIST PUB** at the topic request screen. At the prompt for a subheading, type in the name of the periodical. If that publication is in the *Index*, the complete listing of address, price, etc. will appear.

FAST FWD or **FAST REV** keys allow you to move forward or backward several citations at a time (ten percent of the total number of references in the current citation group). This is useful when you are working with a large number of references.

Quick Guide to Searching PsycLIT on CD-ROM

To Search PsycLIT on Compact disc, you need to know three basic commands:

FIND (**F2**) - to search for a subject or author
SHOW (F4) - to look at the results of a search
PRINT (F6) - to print the citations and/or abstracts for items you wish to use

You may also want to use the following:

ESC	for a menu of commands at any time
HELP (F1)	for help on current function or menu of help topics
INDEX (F5)	to look up terms in and select terms from the alphabetical index for searching
RESTART (F7)	to end you search session or start over
EXCHANGE (F8)	to move form one PsycLIT disc to another
ESC-C	to clear the Find workspace

```
HOW TO SEARCH
```

To search, PRESS F2 - FIND; then type in your subject.
For example, type in: first impressions.

The screen will respond with a set of search results including the number of items in the database containing your search term (known as "hits"). Use F2 -FIND any time you want to return to your search screen to add to or refine your search.

```
SilverPlatter 1.6        PsycLIT Disc 2 (1/83 - 9/89)      Esc=Commands F1=Help

  No.     Records   Request

  #1:       5183    FIRST
  #2:        606    IMPRESSIONS
  #3:         31    FIRST IMPRESSIONS



FIND:   first impressions
```

Type search then Enter (⏎). To see records use Show (F4). To Print use (F6).

```
HOW TO SHOW YOUR RESULTS
```

To look at the results, press F4 - SHOW, then RETURN. The first record will be displayed. Items are displayed in reverse chronological order. Use F10 for NEXT RECORD, F9 for PREVIOUS RECORD, and PGDN, PGUP for multiple screens. On scratch paper jot down record numbers you would like to print, e.g. 2 Of 32.

A sample record from PsycLIT looks like this:

```
SilverPlatter 1.6        PsycLIT Disc 2 (1/83 - 9/89)      Esc=Commands F1=Help
                                                                     2 of 31
 TI: Interpersonal similarity and the social and intellectual dimensions of
     first impressions.
 AU: Lydon,-John-E.; Jamieson,-David-W.; Zanna,-Mark-P.
 IN: U Waterloo, ON, Canada
 JN: Social-Cognition; 1988 Vol 6(4) 269-286
 IS: 0278016X
 LA: English
 PY: 1988
 AB: 89 undergraduates were asked to form social and intellectual first
     impressions of a target person who was similar or dissimilar to them in
     terms of both attitudes and activity preferences. Results indicate that
     both attitude and activity preference similarity affected judgments of
     attraction. However, activity similarity was especially predictive of
     liking judgments, whereas attitude similarity was especially predictive of
     respect judgments. This differential effect was even more pronounced for
     the inference of personality traits. Findings suggest that interpersonal
     similarity and attraction are multidimensional constructs. (PsycLIT
     Database Copyright 1989 American Psychological Assn, all rights reserved)
```

HOW TO PRINT

To PRINT, press F6 - PRINT. First, enter the fields you wish to print. For example CITN, AB will produce article citation and abstract (summary). Next press the TAB key and type in the record numbers desired, separated by commas, e.g. 2,5,9. Last press RETURN to begin printing. Pressing CNTL.BREAK will stop the printer if you make a mistake.

SilverPlatter 1.6   PsycLIT Disc 2 (1/83 - 9/89)   Esc=Commands F1=Help

                                                                      2 of 31
TI: Interpersonal similarity and the social and intellectual dimensions of
    first impressions.
AU: Lydon,-John-E.; Jamieson,-David-W.; Zanna,-Mark-P.
IN: U Waterloo, ON, Canada
JN: Social-Cognition; 1988 Vol 6(4) 269-286
IS: 0278016X
LA: English
PY: 1988
AB: 89 undergraduates were asked to form social and intellectual first

---

PRINT Fields: *citn,ab*   Records: *2,5,9*
        separate pages: (No) Yes   searches: (No) Yes
TAB between settings to change; RETURN to start with first record;

IF YOUR SEARCH PRODUCES TOO MANY RECORDS

(1) Try combining two concepts using the word AND
            e.g. ANOREXIA AND SELF-ESTEEM.
        (Anorexia results in 1383 hits; anorexia and self-esteem in 24 hits)
(2) Look for narrower terms in the Thesaurus of Psychological Index Terms or
    in the descriptor field of records found.

IF YOUR SEARCH DOES NOT PRODUCE ENOUGH RECORDS

(1) Try using a broader term E.G. EATING DISORDERS
(2) Search again using synonyms or additional subject terms from the
    Thesaurus or the descriptor field of the records found
(3) Combine terms using the word OR   e.g. ANOREXIA OR BULIMIA (1867 hits)
    combined with SELF-ESTEEM produces 50 hits.

TO SEARCH FOR AN AUTHOR

Use F5 - INDEX. Type in author's last name, followed by first name or initial. SELECT all the varying forms of the name by pressing RETURN each time the light bar is on a line that might be a variant of the author's name (e.g. Bruner-j and bruner-jerome and bruner-jerome s)

When you finish SELECTing, F2 - FIND will create a set of search results for the author including all forms of his/her name. Proceed as above with SHOW and PRINT commands from FIND screen.

TO END YOUR SESSION

Press F7 - RESTART.

Prepared by Emily Camp
March 1990

PsycLIT Subject Search Planning Guide
For Experienced Searchers

Burke Library, Hamilton College

1. State your research question. If you found the ideal article for your research, what would its title be?

For example:
What is the effect of television violence on children's behavior?

2. Analyze your question and break it down into its concepts.

For example:
Concepts for the above research question are:
1) **television,** 2) **children** and 3) **violence.**

Research questions which imply at least two concepts are generally those best suited to a *PsycLIT* search. Searches of single-concept questions often generate too many results and much irrelevant material. If your research questions implies only one concept, you may need to narrow that topic by examining a specific aspect of it. See page 3-3 in the *PsycLIT Manual* for more help in analyzing your topic. If you are having difficulty analyzing your question or narrowing your topic, ask a reference librarian for assistance.

3. Search the *Thesaurus of Psychological Index Terms* for descriptors, or subject terms, relevant to each concept.

For example:
Descriptors that express the concept "television" are: *television, television advertising,*
cartoons (humor), and *mass media.*
Descriptors for "children" are: *children* and *childhood.*
Descriptors for "violence" are: *violence* and *aggressive behavior.*

Pages 3-7 to 3-14 in the *PsycLIT Manual* describe this completely. If you are having difficulty, ask a reference librarian for help.

4. Note any other terms which describe each concept and might be used in authors' titles, in key phrases, or in abstracts.

For example:
tv, violent, aggression, commercials, animated film, etc.

Pages 3-18 to 3-27 of the *PsycLIT Manual* provide a discussion of free-text searching. Ask a reference librarian if you need assistance.

5. Write down search statements using Boolean logical operators and other connectors. Limit searching to specific fields where applicable (e.g. *aggressive-behavior in de*) .

For example:
(tv **OR** television) **AND**
(children **OR** childhood) *in de* **AND**
(violen* **OR** aggressive-behavior *in de*) .

See pages 3-3 to 3-4 in the *PsycLIT Manual* for further explanation. If you have questions, ask a reference librarian.

6. Execute your search in *PsycLIT* Pages 3-5 to 3-7 or the *PsycLIT Manual* as well as the Silver Platter manual *Getting Started* provide detailed instructions. If you have problems, ask a reference librarian for help.

7. If your search results yield too many or too few articles, you will need to modify your search stategy. Broaden your search to increase results by adding descriptor or free-text terms. Narow your search to decrease results by eliminating less relevant terms, limiting searching to specific fields, or adding another concept. Page 3-31 or the *PsycLIT Manual* covers this. If you have questions, ask a reference librarian for help.

2/88
lab

PsycLIT Quick Reference Guide

For Experienced Searchers

Basic Commands

[F1] Help
Learn more about commands and techniques.

[F2] Find
Start a search.
Modify a search.
Return to searching.

[F3] Guide to the Database
Includes sample searches.
Explains *PsycLIT* fields.
Includes a list of stopwords.

[F4] Show
Display search results on the screen.

[F5] Index
View correct form and spelling of authors names.
View subject terms.

[F6] Print
Print search results.

[F7] Restart
End a search session.
Erase all previous work.

[F8] Exchange
Change disks.
Saves your search steps for re-use on the new disk.

Phrase Searching

Example:
empty nest   *Do not hyphenate words in a phrase.*
latchkey children

Multi-word Descriptor Searching

Example:
test-anxiety   *Hyphenate multi-word descriptors.*
human-sex-differences

Word Root Searching

Example:
adolescen*   *retrieves: adolescence, adolescent, and adolescents*

Re-Use Search Terms Using Set Numbers.

Example:
#1: (HOMELESS OR HOMELESSNESS)
#2: CHILDREN
#3: #1 AND #2

Field Searching Using "in"

homelessness **in de**	*in descriptor field*
violence **in ma**	*in major descriptor field*
college students **in kp**	*in key phrase field*
homeless **in tl**	*in title field*
homeless **in ab**	*in abstract field*
journal-of-social-psychology **in jn**	*in a specific journal*
3340 **in cc**	*as a classification code*
human **in po**	*in population field*

MULTIPLE FIELD SEARCHING

Examples:
(college-students in de) or (college students in kp)
(homeless in ti) or (homeless in ab) or
(homelessness in de)

AUTHOR SEARCHES

1. Look up the author's name in the **INDEX**.
   a. Press: **[F5]**
   b. Enter author's name: **singer-j**
   c. Note the correct form of the author's name.

2. Enter the correct form of the author's name.
   a. Press: **[F2]**
   b. Enter author's name: **singer-jerome-l in au**

LIMIT YOUR SEARCH

By Language

#5 and english in la	English language only
#5 and (english in la or french in la)	English or French

By Publication Year

#6 and py=1987	1987 only
#6 and py=1976-1988	between 1976 and 1988
#4 and py>=1976	1976 and later
#4 and py<=1988	1988 and earlier

SHOW RESULTS ON THE SCEEN   [F4]

A. Display *all* fields for *all* records retrieved.
   1. Press: **[F4]**
   2. Press: **[Return]**

SHOW Fields: **ALL**	Records: **ALL**

B. Display *specific* fields and records.
   1. Press: **[F4]**
   2. Use **TAB** key to move to Fields/Records and change the display formats.
   3. Press: **[Return]**

SHOW Fields: **ti,de,ab**	Records: **1-20**

PRINT SEARCH RESULTS   [F6]

A. Print *citations* for *all* records retrieved.
   1. Press: **[F6]**
   2. Press: **[Return]**

PRINT Fields: **CITN**	Records: **ALL**

B. Print *specific* fields and records.
   1. Press: **[F6]**
   2. Use **TAB** key to move to Fields/Records and change the print formats.
   3. Press: **[Return]**

PRINT Fields: **all**	Records: **1,3,6-8**

PRINT SEARCH HISTORY WITH CITATIONS:

1. Press: **[F6]**
2. Specify Print fields and records.
3. Use **TAB** key to change **searches: (No)** to **"Yes"**.

PRINT Fields: **CITN**	Records: **ALL**
separate pages: (No)Yes	**searches:** (No)Yes

PRINT OR SHOW AN EARLIER SEARCH SET.

1. Enter set number: **#5**
2. Press: **[Return]**
3. Enter Print **[F6]** or Show **[F4]** command.

Hamilton College Library
Clinton, N.Y 13323

Boolean Logical Operators

Or	And	Not

Or

Use to combine synonyms. This will retrieve articles that contain either the word TV or television.

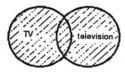

TV OR television

And

This will retrieve articles that contain both words, televsion and children.

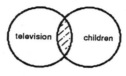

television AND children

Not

This will retrieve articles that contain the word television, but will exclude all articles that contain the word advertising. Use with caution. You might eliminate relevant articles.

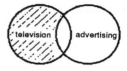

television NOT advertising

Putting your search together using Boolean operators:

1.

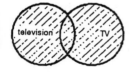

television OR TV = set #1

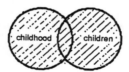

childhood OR children = set #2

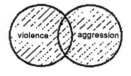

violence OR aggression = set #3

2.

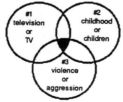

#1 AND #2 AND #3

| Middlebury College | Newspaper Abstracts Ondisc |
| Library | |

Introduction

Newspaper Abstracts Ondisc indexes and abstracts articles from recent issues of these newspapers, all of which are available in the Library:

New York Times   Chicago Tribune
Wall Street Journal   Christian Science Monitor
Washington Post   Los Angeles Times
Boston Globe   Atlanta Constitution

The database may be searched by any **keyword** in the citations, including titles, subjects, names, and abstracts (summaries/descriptions of the articles).

Getting started

Move to the opening menu for Newspaper Abstracts Ondisc

if a previous search is on the screen;

press **\<F10\>**   *\<function key 10\> to back up to the menu;*
type **Y**   *in answer to the prompt to Restart (Y,N)?*
press\<up\> *or* \<down\> arrow keys to highlight the option

| SEARCH UMI Newspaper Abstracts Ondisc |

press **\<Enter\>**   *same as the* **\<Return\>** *key*

Search by keyword

The system prompts for your search term(s).
Enter the term(s) you wish to find and then press **\<Enter\>** (**\<Return\>** key).

| Search term(s): _____ |

Description	*Command*	*Example*
Search		
for a word	*term(s)*	CHINA
for a title	**TI**(*term*)	TI(BUDDHISM)
for an author	**AU**(*term*)	AU(KISSINGER)
for a subject	**SU**(*term*)	SU(PETROLEUM)
for a name as subject	**PN**(*term*)	PN(THATCHER)
for a company	**CO**(*term*)	CO(MOBILE)
Combine search terms		
and previous search results		
find both terms	*term1* **AND** *term2*	CHINA AND COMMUNISM
find either term	*term1* **OR** *term2*	CHINA OR CHINESE
find 1st term, not 2nd	*term1* **AND NOT** *term2*	CHINA AND NOT TAIWAN
combine search sets	*[#]* **AND/OR/AND NOT** *[#]*	[1] AND [2]
Truncate		
a word ending	**?**	COMMUNIS?
View words indexed		
enter word	*term*	BUDDHISM *(do not press \<Enter\>)*
see index listing	press **\<F6\>**	\<function key 6\> at top of keyboard

Select the Newspapers you wish to search

all newspapers	press **\<Enter\>**	"Search All Newspaper Indexes" highlighted
specific newspapers	press **\<up\>** *or* **\<down\>**	arrow keys to highlight specific newspapers
	press **\<space bar\>**	to select/deselect a specified newpaper
	press **\<Enter\>**	when finished selecting newspaper(s)

View search results

view article titles	press <Enter>	after system shows it has results from your search
move through list	press <up> *or* <down>	arrow keys
select citations to print	press <F9>	<function key 9>

view full citations	press <Enter>	display full citation for current/highlighted citation
move through list	press <+> *or* <->	keys on keypad on right side of keyboard
select citations to print	press <F9>	<function key 9>

Print citations

print command	press <F4>	<function key 4> *a new window opens:*

Output options

choose print format	press <up> *or* <down>	arrow keys to highlight options for printing with either long or short citations
	press <space bar>	to save your choice
	press <Enter>	to continue *a new window opens:*

What do you want to output?

choose citations to be printed	press <up> *or* <down>	arrow keys to highlight options for printing marked (selected), current, or all citations
	press <Enter>	to begin printing

Download citations

Citations may be saved to an IBM-formatted disk (Mac disks will not work).
- Follow the above procedures for Printing, but within "Output Options" select ouput to *Disk file.*

Changing discs for different years of Newspaper Abstracts Ondisc

Not all the citations for Newspaper Abstracts fit onto a single compact disc. There are discs for
    1985-86   1989-90
    1987-88

To search for citations from a different year, you must change discs in the CD-ROM player.

        press <Alt> *and* <F10>   *a new window opens:*

Change Disc

- Note directions on the screen.
- Press the "Eject" button on the NEC CD-ROM player, remove the disc, and place the disc you wish to search in the player. *You do not have to take the compact discs out of the plastic cases!!!*
- Wait a few seconds for the new disc to load, and then begin a new search.
- When you are finished, *please repeat this procedure and return the most recently dated disc to the player.*

Function key summary

Help	<F1>
Show function keys	<F2>
Enter new search	<F3>
Print	<F4>
Word index	<F6>
Mark item to print	<F9>
Start over	<F10>
Change discs	<Alt><F10>

9/90jr

REDEEMER COLLEGE LIBRARY

PsycLIT

BEFORE YOU BEGIN, PLAN YOUR SEARCH STRATEGY BY FILLING IN A PSYCLIT SEARCH PLANNER (located by computer terminal).

There are three ways to access the various functions on PsycLIT: (1) choose from the menu; (2) use functions keys; (3) press ESCAPE and the first letter of the command you wish to use e.g. F for FIND.

The two basic functions of PsycLIT include searching for records (FIND) and displaying records found (SHOW).

SEARCHING: FIND (F2)

> You may search using....
>> a descriptor (subject term found in the thesaurus)-----> **visual-perception**
>> a word-----> **bulimia**
>> a word phrase-----> **empty nest**
>> an author-----> **Benner-David**   *NOTE: Be sure to use the INDEX function on PsycLIT when searching an author's name (see below).
>> a previous search statement-----> **#19**

NOTE: Use hyphens to connect words in the descriptor and author fields as indicated.

Combining Concepts

Use **AND** to narrow a search.

Use **OR** to broaden a search.

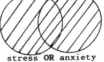

creativity **AND** children

stress **OR** anxiety

Narrowing the Search

Broadening the Search

Use **AND** to add more concepts ------ Eliminate a concept
Eliminate **OR's** -------------------- Use **OR's** to include synonymns/related
terms.
Do not truncate -------------------- Truncate e.g. **bulimi*** picks up the
words **bulimia, bulimic, bulimics.**
Limit search terms to certain ----- Extend search to basic index
fields e.g. **visual-perception in de**   e.g. **visual perception**

111

DISPLAYING RECORDS FOUND: SHOW (F4)

You will see the following on the screen:
FIELDS:ALL   RECORDS:ALL

Type over the word ALL after FIELDS if you want to see specific FIELDS only, e.g. (1) citn, ab (citation, abstract): (2) ti,de (title, descriptor).
Type over the word ALL after RECORDS if you want to see a sample of the RECORDS found, e.g. (1) 1-5: (2) 1,5,10,15,25.

BROWSING INDEX TERMS: INDEX (F5)

Using this function allows you to browse and select the terms you wish to use in your search. It is especially valuable for searching by author because one can never be sure how an author's name has been entered in the database.

DOWNLOADING/TRANSFERRING RECORDS TO FLOPPY DISK

This function copies your search results onto a floppy disk.

1. Place a formatted floppy disk into the floppy disk drive. Make sure the drive is closed.

2. Press ESC (Escape) then D for download or choose it from the menu.

3. You will see the following on the screen:
    FIELDS:ALL   RECORDS:ALL

    Type citn,ab over the word ALL after FIELDS. This will eliminate all the unnecessary information.
    Select the records you wish to save to a file on floppy disk by typing in your selection over the word ALL after RECORDS. Do not copy more than 30 records at a time because the file will be too large.

4. Tab over to FILENAME and rename the default filename A:\download.doc by typing over the name e.g., A:\stress. Choose a name that you will remember. You will use it later to retrieve the file you have created.

5. To retrieve the file on another computer, upload the file into a word processing package by calling it up from the directory.

Margaret Noordhof
Public Services Librarian
Dec. 1990/rev

PsycLIT SEARCH PLANNER

This worksheet is designed to help you develop a search strategy before carrying out a search on PsycLIT.

For assistance in finding correct descriptors (subject headings), consult the Thesaurus of Psychological Terms located beside the computer terminal.

****

1.   State your topic in one sentence as completely as you can.
     _____
     _____

2.   Think about your topic and circle the two or three most important concepts.

3.   Write each concept you circled in a top space on the lines below. Then list synonymous or related terms below each, if applicable. Use the thesaurus to find other useful terms.

     First Concept   Second Concept   Third Concept
     _____   _____   _____

OR_____   OR_____   OR_____

OR_____   OR_____   OR_____

OR_____   OR_____   OR_____

     CONNECTORS   __AND__   __AND__

4.   Write out the search statements that you will enter to get your sets.

find_____

find_____

find_____

find_____

Search one concept at a time and keep track of what you type in.

If you need any assistance at any stage of your search, please ask at the Reference Desk.

Margaret Noordhof
Public Services Librarian
Dec. 1990/rev

PsycLIT
GPO
ERIC

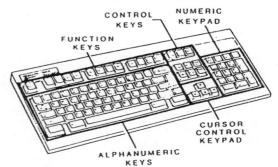

CD ROM User Guide

THE KEYBOARD

Teach yourself about PsycLit	HELP **F1** **F2** FIND	Find words or phrases
Identify searchable fields	GUIDE **F3** **F4** SHOW	Show retrieved records on screen
To browse for author names, journals, and subject words	INDEX **F5** **F6** PRINT	Print retrieved records on paper
Begin or end a session Erase a search	RESTART **F7** **F8** XCHANGE	Does not function
Show previous record	PREVIOUS **F9** **F10** NEXT	Show next record

FUNCTION KEYS

F 2

FIND COMMAND
Press the **F2** key.
After the FIND prompt appears,
type the **subject** or **author** you
wish to search.

To look for:	type:
a word	**dyslexia**
a word phrase	**peer pressure**
a descriptor	**self-esteem in DE**
a descriptor phrase	**self esteem**
a word root	**adolescen***
a search statement	**#2**
a number	**1066**
an author	**Smith-John**
	Smith-John-K
	Smith-J*

To combine concepts
• use **AND** to narrow a search

Citations include both ego AND personality

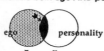

• use **OR** to broaden a search

Citations include either ego OR personality

To limit a search

- You can limit a search to any of the following fields:

TI	Article Title	AN	Abstract Number
AU	Author(s)/Editor(s)	AB	Abstract
JN	Journal Name	DE	Descriptors
LA	Language	PO	Population (human or
PY	Publication Year		animal; only in PsycLIT)

To limit a search to a selected field, use "in" and the field abbreviation.

by author..........................**Skinner in AU**
by language ....**English in LA**
by population..................**human in PO**
by pub date.......................**1984 in PY**
PY>=1986
PY=1980-1987; PY<=1983
by selected fields.............**suicide in TI**
suicide in AB
drug in DE

SHOW COMMAND

F 4

Press the **F4** key to see the records found by your subject or author search. Use the **PageDown** key $\boxed{Pg_{Dn}}$ to move from one **screen** to the next. Use **Previous** $\boxed{F9}$ or **Next** $\boxed{F10}$ to move from **record** to record.

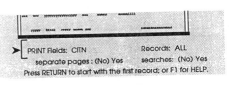

SHOW fields: ALL   Records: ALL
Press PgDn for more; F9 for previous record; F10 for next record; F2 for FIND.

If you do not indicate which **Fields** and **Records** you want to see, the system will automatically show all.

PRINT COMMAND

F 6

This command prints a record. If **CITN** is selected, the system prints **TI, AU, IN, JN,** and **AN** fields. To get all of these fields plus the abstract, type **CITN, AB.**

PRINT Fields: CITN   Records: ALL
separate pages : (No) Yes   searches: (No) Yes
Press RETURN to start with the first record; or F1 for HELP.

You may select specific records to print. Use the tab key $\boxed{\leftrightarrow}$ to move from **Print** fields to **Records.** Then type the **Record Numbers** you need.
Separate pages: Select **NO.**
Searches: Select **YES** to print your search strategy.

To **STOP** ➤ the $\boxed{F2}$ **FIND** or $\boxed{F4}$ **SHOW** or $\boxed{F6}$ **PRINT** action while it is processing, press the $\boxed{Ctrl}$ and $\boxed{Scroll\ Lck/Break}$ keys simultaneously. You may have to repeat this procedure if the system does not respond immediately.

Before beginning a search, please complete a copy of "Preparing for Your CD ROM Tutorial," available at the Information Desk. Need help? Ask at the Information Desk.

LIBRARY INSTRUCTION
PENFIELD LIBRARY • SUNY COLLEGE AT OSWEGO

O. Opello & T. Lundstrom
11-87; rev. 1-88/JF
rev. 5-90

PsycLIT Search Strategy Planner

System Commands

Boolean Logical Operators:
OR, AND, NOT

PsycLIT System Connectors:
WITH, NEAR, IN, =

1. What is your research question? _____

2. List the concepts of your question:

CONCEPT 1	CONCEPT 2	CONCEPT 3

3. Use the *Thesaurus of Psychological Index Terms* to find descriptors which describe each concept:

CONCEPT 1		CONCEPT 2		CONCEPT 3
OR _____ OR _____	AND	OR _____ OR _____	AND	OR _____ OR _____

4. Add other terms relevant to each concept which an author might use in a title:

OR _____ OR _____	AND	OR _____ OR _____	AND	OR _____ OR _____

5. Write down the search statements to be entered on the *PsycLIT* computer:

1. _____
2. _____
3. _____
4. _____
5. _____

EVALUATION FORMS

Eastern Oregon State College

CD-ROM QUESTIONNAIRE

1. Which of our CD ROM databases are you evaluating?

2. Have you ever used a computer to search for information?
   Yes   No

3. Have you ever used a personal computer before?   Yes   No

4. Was the system easy to learn?   Yes   No

5. Was the system easy to use once you had learned to use it?
   Yes   No

6. What kind of assistance did you use to learn the system? (Circle more than one if appropriate)

   HelpScreen   Manual   Librarian   Friend   None

7. If you received assistance, was it useful?

Help Screen	Yes	No	No Opinion
Manual	Yes	No	No Opinion
Librarian	Yes	No	No Opinion

8. Did you receive relevant citations?   Yes   No

9. Was the search completed within a reasonable amount of time?
   Yes   No

10. What is your status?
    Falculty   Staff   Student   Other

11. What are your opinions of the display and print capabilities of the system? (Use back side if needed)

issued 9/15/89

119